# CHILD
# DEVELOPMENT
# & THE FAMILY

# CHILD DEVELOPMENT & THE FAMILY

J. Jupe
E. Powell
V. Powell
M. Bishop
and C. Owen

Selected photographs by John and Penny Hubley

## MACMILLAN EDUCATION

First published 1985
Reprinted 1986, 1987

Published by
MACMILLAN EDUCATION LTD
Houndmills, Basingstoke, Hampshire RG21 2XS
and London
Companies and representatives
throughout the world

Printed in Hong Kong

ISBN 0-333-32171-5

*Consultants Dr Penelope and Dr John Hubley.*

# Acknowledgements

The author and publishers wish to acknowledge the following photograph sources:

BBC Hulton Picture Library, pp. 12, 13, 14;
Biophoto Associates, p. 60;
Jim Brownbill, pp. 1, 2 *top right*, 3 *top right* and *bottom*, 94;
Camera Press, p. 59;
John Cleare/Mountain Camera, p. 116 *top*;
Colorsport, pp. 4 *centre right*, 115 *centre right*;
Debbie Dooley, p. 23;
Family Planning Association/Cyril Bernard, pp. 40, 41, 42;
Henry Grant, p. 73;
Sally and Richard Greenhill, cover illustration, *second row right*, pp. 2 *bottom*, 4 *top left* and *bottom*, 8, 27 *left*, 49, 61 *right*, 63, 70, 71, 74, 86, 115 *bottom right*, 121 *top*, 129;
Harry F Harlow, University of Wisconsin Primate Laboratory, p. 102;
Health Education Council, p. 57
John and Penny Hubley, cover illustrations, pp. 2 *top left*, 4 *top right*, 5, 7, 9, 10, 17, 20, 27 *right*, 29, 61 left, 67, 75, 76, 77, 78, 84, 85, 89, 90, 91, 96, 106, 112, 113, 114, 115 *top*, *centre left* and *bottom left*, 116 *bottom*, 117, 118, 119, 120, 121 *bottom*, 125, 126, 127, 128, 130, 131;
Camilla Jessel, pp. 36, 50, 68, 88, 98, 101, 109;
Sheelah Latham, pp. 3 *top left*, 123;
M. 4 Design, p. 6;
Maggie Murray/Format, p. 19;
NSPCC, p. 107;
Popperfoto, p. 24;
Carlos Reyes, p. 4 *centre left*;
ROSPA, p. 94;
Standard Telephone Cables Ltd, p. 16 *bottom*;
Thomson Holidays, p. 116 *centre*;
Jim Turner, pp. 18, 95;
C James Webb, pp. 35, 58;
Norman White, p. 51.

The publishers have made every effort to trace the copyright holders, but where they have failed to do so they will be pleased to make the necessary arrangements at the first opportunity.

# Contents

# Preface

Very few people are lucky enough to have a biography written about themselves. Yet probably each of us would like to know what it is that has influenced the kind of person we are.

Most of the readers of this book will become parents. The task of parenting is probably the greatest responsibility any individual undertakes. Parents have the most significant effect in developing their child's potential. They influence the intellectual, physical, social and emotional development of their child.

What is a family? How does life begin? How do children develop? This book helps to answer some of these questions.

The five authors have been influenced in its compilation by a range of experiences and skills drawn from parenthood; the study of the psychology of childhood; curriculum development, tutoring secondary school pupils; and the teaching of child development, home economics and sociology.

We would like to thank all the parents and children we have met who have taught us so much about human development.

Edwina Powell

# 1 Families

## Introducing us!

Human babies, unlike animals, take a long time to grow up. In fact they remain dependent upon their parents until they are at least sixteen years of age. The laws of our society reflect this: school is compulsory in Britain until a boy or girl reaches sixteen years of age; nobody may marry until they are sixteen years of age, and then only wth the consent of their parents.

Can you think of other adult rights which an individual does not attain until the age of sixteen years or eighteen years?

Human babies and children need a lot of care. The parents in the photograph above have nearly finished their task of caring for and bringing up their children. At first their babies were totally dependent upon them. Only the parents (or other adults in charge) could meet their needs. The babies were incapable of doing anything for themselves except to communicate their basic needs.

**Changes then begin to happen quickly.**

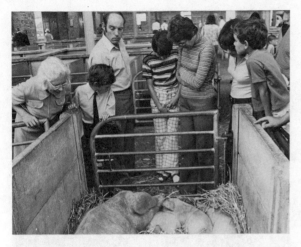

During each stage of their growing up they are being prepared for the next stage.

**What kinds of feelings do you think the parents have about their children growing up?**

By the time these children are teenagers they are becoming more independent and self-reliant. They are now adolescent, their bodies and feelings are changing and developing rapidly. They are passing from childhood towards adulthood.

**'Now I hardly see them except when they are hungry or need money.'**

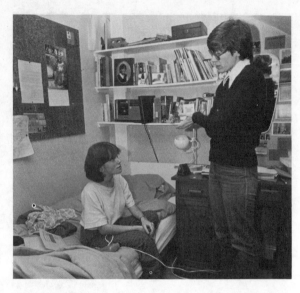

What kinds of feelings do you think the adolescents have in each of these situations?

In the situations shown, young people are expected to behave in a certain way. Sometimes the way our friends expect us to behave is not the way our parents and teachers expect.

Describe the expectations of
  1 parents/teachers
  2 friends
in each case.

Since birth these young people have developed in many ways.

1 Their behaviour towards people has changed. They have developed socially.
2 Their bodies have changed and developed. They have developed physically.
3 Their feelings about themselves and other people have changed. They have developed emotionally.
4 Their ability to think and understand has developed. They have developed intellectually. At one time they could only count

using their fingers. Now they can probably solve problems using symbols, e.g. $x^2 - 2x + 1 = 0$.

Many factors will have influenced their development — parents, school, friends (peers), TV and magazines — but their family will have played the most important part in shaping their development.

## Family groups

The smallest family unit is called a *nuclear* or *conjugal* family and it consists of a woman, a man, and their children or child. The *extended* family is a larger grouping. It consists of people related to each other by descent, marriage and adoption and it often spans three generations. So, it includes uncles, aunts, cousins and grandparents. The extended family is made up of a series of nuclear families that are related to each other. It is not necessary for all the family members to live together in the same house in order for it to be an extended family.

## Families in different societies

Many advertisements and stories describe a family as two parents living with their

children in the same house. According to these images, when the children are old enough to live independently, they leave home and start their own families. This is not the only type of family though.

Have you ever written an essay entitled 'My Family'? It is very likely that you have, at least once during your school life. You may have described your parents, brothers and sisters and grandparents. If you had read the essays written by your classmates you would probably have found that different pupils had different families from yours. Some families may include a grandparent while others have only the parents and children. Many children live with only one parent. Some people live in the same neighbourhood as aunts, uncles and grandparents while others may live many miles from their relatives.

If children in different parts of the world wrote about their families, their essays would also be very different from yours. In some parts of the world the family group is not made up of a mother, father, sons and daughters. Amongst the Ashanti people in Ghana, a husband and wife may live in separate houses for many years, or all their lives. The mother takes her new baby to her own village to live with her parents, rather than form a new family group with the child's father. In some places the father may see his eldest son as a rival and he may be sent to live with his grandparents. The traditional family in India is made up of the head of the household and his wife, their sons and daughters-in-law and grandchildren. This is called a joint family and they live in the same house and work together on the family's land. It is not until their parents die that the sons go to live in separate homes with their wives and children.

In Tibet when a woman marries the eldest son in a family, she may be expected to treat all her husband's brothers like her own husband. When this happens all the men accept equal responsibility for any children that are born. In other societies the chief man may have up to fifty or one hundred wives. In 1953, the chief of the Swazi tribe in Southern Africa had fifty-six wives.

These are examples of families in different societies. A society is a group of people who live in the same place. The members of a society have similar habits, customs and beliefs and there are rules which most people obey. A society is usually made up of a large number of people. In many cases a country may be a society. However, some societies may be small like that of the Kalahari bushmen. The customs, beliefs and rules of different societies mean that families in different societies are not the same.

As families in different parts of the world are so different from each other, is it possible to give one definition that covers all families everywhere? We can say that a family is a group of people who are related to each other by blood or by marriage. The family members are seen by themselves and by other people in society, as a separate group in the society in which they live.

## What do all families have in common?

Although family groups are different all over the world, they all have some common functions. Some of the family's jobs and responsibilities are:

1 reproduction: the birth of children
2 socialisation of children
3 economic support
4 emotional support and care
5 sexual relationships

### 1 Reproduction

At birth a baby is very helpless and will take many years to grow up and become independent. It is usually the family that provides the

care and shelter the baby needs. The parents and adult relatives in the family usually take on the main responsibility for this, but sometimes older brothers and sisters help to care for the young child.

### 2 Socialisation of children

Families prepare children to take their place in society. Living within his family a child learns the language and way of life of his society. He comes to know its rules and what it expects of him. This process of learning how to behave to fit into society is called *socialisation*. Within the family socialisation takes place in two ways. First, from deliberate teaching by the adults and second, from their setting an example for the children to follow.

### 3 Economic support

In industrialised countries it is usual for one or both parents to earn money to buy the goods and services the family needs. Sometimes economic support stretches beyond the immediate family to other relatives. For many families in developing countries the position is very different. There the family members may work together on the land they own or rent. By their combined efforts they grow their own food. They sell some of the food they grow in order to buy other goods they do not produce themselves, like clothes, agricultural tools and cooking utensils.

Providing economic support for the whole family involves the strong and fit members. People who need to rely on those members of the family for economic support are called *dependants*. Children, the elderly and sick are usually dependants, though sometimes they too make a financial contribution to the family.

### 4 Emotional support and care

One of the most important jobs of the family is to provide emotional support, protection and security for its members. Relationships with workmates, schoolfriends, or neighbours are usually different from family

relationships. Parents show their love and affection for their children by bringing them up as best they can and protecting and caring for them. Then when the parents become elderly and the children are mature, many children will care for the parents and protect them.

## 5 Sexual relationships

Many societies consider that a sexual relationship should only take place between husband and wife. In some societies, a couple having a sexual relationship outside marriage may receive severe punishment and be rejected by their families.

Even in developed countries like Britain and France, where views on sexual relationships have changed considerably over the last few decades, many people disapprove of sexual freedom on moral or religious grounds. In most of these societies there are still rules forbidding or limiting sexual activity outside marriage. For example, in Britain it is illegal to have sexual intercourse with someone who is less than sixteen years old. Young people cannot marry by law until they are sixteen years old. Even then, they need the consent of their parents.

In most societies the idea of 'inheritance' is very important. There are many rules that govern who should inherit from the parents when they die. Often the rules of inheritance allow only *legitimate* children or even only the eldest sons to inherit. Legitimate children are children born into a family recognised by that society. In this way society reinforces the idea of restricting sexual relations to marriage.

## Are there families in all societies?

Societies all over the world can be very different from each other. Do all societies have families in them though? In 1949 a sociologist called George Murdock made a study to find out whether there were any societies which did not have families. He wanted to find out if all societies had recognised family groups which performed some or all of the functions described above. He studied 250 societies, from small hunting and gathering tribes to large modern countries. His results showed that some form of family group existed in all these different societies. Sometimes there were individual people who did not have a family, because all their relations had died. Murdock also thought that families would always exist however technologically advanced societies became in the future.

As a result of his study Murdock wrote the

following definition to include all the different families he studied.

'A family is a social group characterised by common residence, economic co-operation and reproduction. It includes adults of both sexes, at least two of whom maintain a socially approved sexual relationship and one or more children owned or adopted by the sexually cohabiting adults.'

To understand this more easily we can make a list of the main points in the definition:

1 families live together
2 families include at least one man and one woman
3 families support their members financially
4 two adults have a socially acceptable sexual relationship
5 families include children

---

**This definition was written in 1949. Do you think it is still valid today in your society? Make a list of the points that you think are true today.**

---

**This family tree shows an extended family.**

In some families children live with only one parent. Their mother or father may be divorced, separated, widowed or unmarried. These families are called one-parent families.

An extended family in the UK.

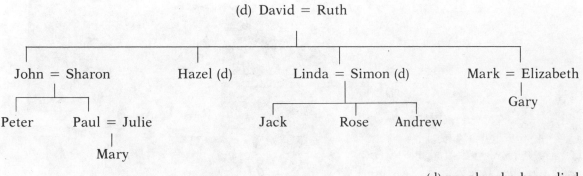

(d) David = Ruth

John = Sharon    Hazel (d)    Linda = Simon (d)    Mark = Elizabeth

Peter    Paul = Julie    Jack    Rose    Andrew    Gary

Mary

(d) people who have died

---

**Can you answer the following questions?**

1 **What relation is John to David?**
2 **What relation is Rose to Ruth?**
3 **What relation is Sharon to David and Ruth?**

4 **What relation would Paul have been to Hazel?**
5 **How many nuclear families are contained in this extended family?**
6 **Are there any one-parent families?**
7 **How many generations are there?**

## Families in traditional societies

In pre-industrial societies the extended family was and is the most usual type of family group. In the 1930s the Kgatla tribe of Botswana in Africa were typical of this kind of family organisation. Traditionally, the extended family could include two or more related nuclear families as well as other relatives. They lived, worked and played together. They produced most of their own food, clothes and tools. In this society the family was a *production unit*. The male head of the household had authority over all other members of the family. This type of society is known as a *patriarchal* society. Everybody in the household had their own specific job to do. This could be fetching water, herding cattle or building or repairing huts. Jobs that were too large for a household on its own were carried out with the help of relatives. Many changes have taken place in the Kgatla way of life since the 1930s, but there are still many societies like this around the world today.

Family relationships are very important in pre-industrial societies. A Pomo Indian of Northern California tried to explain the difference between the family in his small society and the family in the large, modern American society near by. He said, 'What is a man? A man is nothing. Without his family he is of less importance than that bug crossing the trail. In the white ways of doing things the family is not so important. The police and soldiers take care of protecting you, the courts give you justice, the post office carries messages for you, the school teaches you. Everything is taken care of, even your children, if you die; but with us the family must do all of that.'

## Families in changing societies

Changes in societies all over the world have affected traditional extended family groups. The search for work has meant that many people have moved from country areas to towns and cities. Moving away from where

An extended family in India.

they were brought up has affected the relationships between members of the extended family. So too have the different types of housing, such as modern flats, that many governments provide for their people. As a result the nuclear family is becoming increasingly important all over the world.

---

**Make a list of ways in which the extended family can help support a nuclear family. You might think of weddings, providing a home and the birth of a baby, among other examples.**

---

## The changing British family

Families are not fixed and unchanging. As circumstances and societies change, families may change too. Over the last two hundred years British society has changed a great deal and these changes have affected families in three main ways:

1 type of family grouping
2 functions of the family
3 size of families

### 1 Type of family grouping

Modern research has shown that extended families were quite rare in Britain, even before the Industrial Revolution in the mid-eighteenth century. Many families did have adults who were not relatives living with them though. In rich families, these adults were servants. In less wealthy families, the adults were farm workers who lived with the family. Even though the nuclear family was most common before the Industrial Revolution, there was more than one pattern of family life. Extended families similar to those of the Kgatla tribe could be found, especially in rural areas. Today in Britain, there are many different types of family. Of these, the nuclear family is still the most common.

More recently another change has been brought about in family grouping in Britain. In the past both divorce and illegitimate children were considered scandalous and shameful. But in the last twenty to thirty years divorce and separation have become easier and more frequent. Unmarried mothers do not feel they have to get married or have their babies adopted. These changes in social attitudes mean that there are more one-parent families in Britain. An important factor in this change is that, by earning their own living, women now can be more independent of men and keep their children themselves. While in most one-parent families it is the mother who lives with the children, in a substantial minority of families it is the father who brings up his children. This shows another change in social attitudes—that men are able to care for young children as well as women.

Changes in British family life have also come about now that Britain is a multi-racial society. Immigrants who have come to Britain in the past twenty years have brought with them their own customs and attitudes to family life. People of Asian origin consider family ties to be extremely important and show considerable help and support for the members of their extended families. They look after the elderly family members and often live together in extended family groups.

### 2 Functions of the family

In pre-industrial Britain, the majority of families, both nuclear and extended were *units of production*. This means that all the family members helped to produce the food, clothes and tools which were needed. As a result of industrialisation, the family was no longer a unit of production. Instead family members worked in factories for wages, which were used to buy the goods needed by the family. The family became a *unit of consumption*, paying for and consuming goods made by other people. Nowadays, as we saw earlier, one or both parents go out to work to provide financial support for the family.

The functions of the family have changed in other ways too. Over the past hundred years governments have provided more help and services to families. In doing so, the government has started to share some of the responsibilities that the family used to bear by itself. Before the Industrial Revolution it was the family that had complete responsibility for the education and training for work of the younger members of the family. Families had to pay to have their children educated, or teach them themselves or rely on charities. In 1870 compulsory elementary education was introduced and since then the government has taken over more and more responsibility for educating and training children and young people. While the family no longer carries the complete responsibility for education, its contribution is still extremely important. The sections on play and language in this book show that parents take a vital part in the education of pre-school children.

The introduction of the welfare state in Britain in 1944 also meant that the government started to give more help to families.

The National Health Service provides good health care for children. By giving certain grants and allowances the government helps provide financial support for families. This is particularly important for less well-off families.

---

**Make a list of the ways in which the welfare state helps people today. Ask your parents and friends to help. Think particularly about pregnant women, children, sick people and the elderly.**

---

### 3 Size of families

In the nineteenth century working-class families often had from six to ten or more children and middle-class families had an average of six children. Far more babies died during the pregnancy and in infancy than do today. Many of these deaths were due

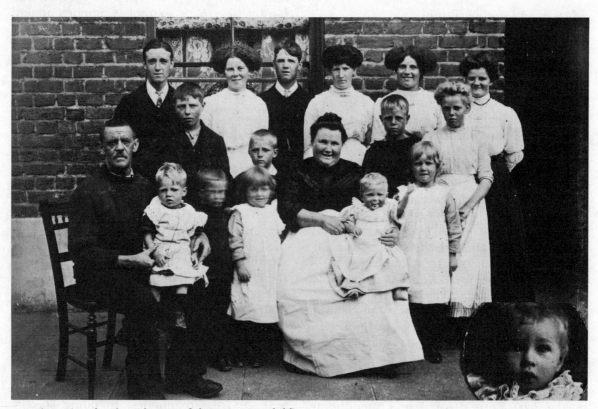

A working-class family with some of their nineteen children.

A middle-class family with six children *c.* 1860.

to bad nutrition, bad housing conditions, poor medical help and a lack of knowledge. Since then however, because of the welfare state and improved medical care, babies have a much better chance of survival.

The average size of a nuclear family in Britain today is two adults with two or three children. The reduction in the size of families has taken place since about 1870. Smaller families originated in the middle classes. The cost of living increased enormously in the second half of the nineteenth century. It became necessary for children to have academic qualifications in order to get similar jobs to their parents. Private schools were started up. Middle-class couples decided to limit the size of their families since they could only afford to educate two or three children.

Working-class families followed this trend towards the end of the century. In 1870 compulsory elementary education for all children meant that children were not allowed to work to help support the family. Feeding and clothing them also became more and more expensive.

During this period the means of limiting families by birth control also became more widely available. In 1877 Annie Besant and Charles Bradlaugh were tried in court for publishing pamphlets on birth control. The trial received enormous publicity. More people began to ask and find out about contraception. Another development of the early twentieth century was rubber technology which enabled effective contraceptives to be produced cheaply.

During the early years of the twentieth century, Mrs Pankhurst led the movement

Women suffragettes in 1912.

for 'Votes for Women'. Women began to ask questions and demand rights. One of the things they demanded was the right to choose whether to have children and how many. This was another factor which led to the reduction in the size of families.

## Are families necessary in any society?

We have seen the way that a family pattern can change over the years. However, despite all the social changes, most people in the world still live in family groups. Families continue to fulfil important social functions concerned with child rearing and emotional and financial support of their members. Yet some people do choose not to live in families. We shall look at two alternatives to the family:

1 communes
2 kibbutzim

### Communes

During recent years some people have decided that a traditional family group does not suit them and they have formed or joined communes. A commune is a group of people who all live together. They share their possessions and activities, and care for each other. A commune can be any size from as small as eight to over four hundred people. In a commune people may be married, living together or single, but they work for the commune as a whole, not just for themselves or their family. Everyone is expected to share fully in the life of the commune. Usually the people will eat together, perhaps work together too, but they generally have a room of their own as well as the use of shared lounges and dining-rooms.

People join communes for a variety of reasons. Some people prefer to share their lives with many people rather than just the immediate family. Some believe that children will benefit from having a close relationship with many adults, rather than just their parents. Communes have been set up all over the world, but statistics show that many of them do not last for more than a few years.

### Kibbutzim

In Israel, communes known as kibbutzim have been set up for many years as an alternative to the traditional pattern of family life. Roughly four per cent of Israel's population live in about 240 kibbutzim settlements. A kibbutz can consist of only a few people or many hundred. The members generally work on the land. Couples may live together by sharing a room if they wish. They can choose whether or not to marry and whether or not to have children.

Kibbutz children do not usually share a room with their parents. When they are a few days old they are taken to join all the other kibbutz children in the Children's House. Here they are brought up by nurses and teachers. This means that both parents are free to do their share of the work for the kibbutz. Children may spend afternoons and evenings with their parents. Kibbutz parents generally believe though, that the proper place for children is with other children of the same age rather than in a family group. Children of the same age are called a child's *peer group*. All the adults, with or without children, feel responsible for the kibbutz children. They call them 'our children'.

All kibbutz children are treated equally. No child has more money or better clothes than any other and they do not seem to be jealous of each other. They are not possessive about their things. This may be because everything belongs to everybody and not to any individuals.

However there may be disadvantages to bringing up children on a kibbutz. People say that kibbutz children find it very difficult to develop deep, loving relationships when they grow up. They are said to be unable to show their emotions very easily. It is thought this may be because they have not experienced the close relationship of their parents directly. Kibbutz children are also said to be less creative and individualistic than children brought up in more traditional family groups. It is argued that the reason for this is that the peer group expects all its members to share the same values and attitudes. A child who does not conform to the peer group is likely to be rejected. Since the kibbutz child spends much time with his or her peer group, rejection would be a miserable experience.

It is very difficult to generalise about the advantages and disadvantages of living on a kibbutz. There is little evidence to prove whether people develop differently or not.

Personal

## COMMUNE CUM STUDY CENTRE 50 MILES FROM LONDON SEEKS NEW MEMBERS

We are a cosmopolitan, socialist group of 18 adults and 15 kids living on a former country estate comprising a 50-roomed mansion, 2 houses, a very large stable block and 17 acres. Age spread: 1-55. Most of us are lecturers, teachers, film-makers and social workers. We also run courses and conferences here. Course interests include: communal living, feminism, co-ops, environmental politics, community action, AT, social science, alternative education, T'ai chi and organic gardening. Available space: one 4 roomed and one 2 roomed unit.

---

**Imagine that you wish to join the commune. Write a letter saying why you would like to join. Say why you think you might be suitable. Explain why you think commune life might be better than ordinary family life.**

**Or, imagine that you are a reporter or news-broadcaster. Write an article or make a tape recording in which you describe the commune and interview some of the people living there.**

---

## The role of women in British society

In the past most women would have made an essential contribution to the family finances. With the onset of the Industrial Revolution, working-class women continued to be essential to the economic well-being of the family. They worked in the factories and their wages helped to fight against poverty. Middle-class women on the other hand were cut off from the world of work after the Industrial Revolution. Amongst the middle classes work was considered to be a male activity. Women supervised the running of the household. Working-class women worked long hours whilst their middle-class counterparts had to find things to do to occupy themselves.

Nevertheless, the start of the movement for women's equality with men began in the middle-class drawing-room rather than on the shop floor of the factory. There was a drastic shortage of marriageable men after the First World War and this meant that some middle-class women were destined to be a financial drain on their parents for life. These women began to demand that girls as well as boys should receive a formal education and earn their own living. Eventually, schools, colleges and even universities were opened for women. Once women had gained the right to education, they began to demand political *suffrage*, or the right to vote. However, it was not until 1928 that women gained equal voting rights with men.

---

**The Women's Suffrage movement was led by Mrs Pankhurst. Go to your library and find out how she and the suffragettes conducted their campaign to get the vote. What did Emily Davison do at the Derby in 1913?**

---

Over the years women have continued to work for their rights. There are two areas of major concern to women which also influence the family. These are:

1 work
2 the conflicts between child care and employment

### 1 Women at work

Women form about forty per cent of the labour force in Britain. About eighty per cent

Nursing can be seen as an extension of a woman's traditional role as a housewife and mother.

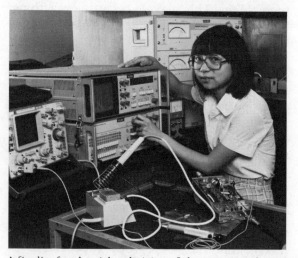

A finalist for the girl technician of the year award.

of the employed women work full time. Two-thirds of women workers are married. Today statistics show that women marry quite soon after they complete school or college; usually the first child is born shortly after marriage. However, the use of the contraceptive pill has allowed more women to delay starting a family in order that they may first establish themselves in a career.

Families are smaller and so women spend less time actually bearing children. Bringing up children is over sooner too, leaving many years for a woman to work, even if she spends several years at home while her children are at school. Now, one third of all mothers are employed outside the home. In addition to these it is difficult to estimate how many women work at home doing jobs like copy-typing or dressmaking.

Despite the Equal Pay Act (1978) women still earn on average far less than men. It is estimated that women outnumber men by a ratio of 5 to 1 in the low paid sector of society. The Sex Discrimination Act (1975) was designed to give women equal rights in employment. However, not many women are found in top professional jobs, e.g. as judges, surgeons or architects. Few women are employed in management positions in industry. They still tend to be in jobs which are fairly similar to women's traditional housewife and mothering role, such as primary school teaching, nursing, secretarial work or the clothing and food processing industries.

However, women are now being actively encouraged to train for 'non-traditional' roles in science and engineering and the new information technology in order to realise their full potential.

### 2 The conflicts between child care and employment

There are still many pressures put upon women to remain at home with their children. This is particularly true in times of economic recession when unemployment is high. Working mothers are often made to feel guilty by statements declaring that their children will be emotionally deprived and that 'latch-key' children become truants and delinquents. There is no evidence to support this view. Pearl Jephcott in her study of women workers in a biscuit factory in Bermondsey found no evidence of child neglect.

Neither did she find any association between delinquency and working mothers. It appeared too, that children preferred their mothers to work.

A boy getting his own tea.

There are few day-care services provided by local authorities. In 1970, for instance, there were only places for less than one per cent of the under-fives in England. This could be interpreted as a lack of official support for working mothers. When mothers do work, it is they, not the fathers, who will typically take time off work to look after a sick child. Although husbands and wives increasingly treat marriage as a partnership, when a mother works she can often find that she has two demanding jobs to her husband's one.

**Should mothers of young children go out to work? Ask your teacher to arrange a debate for you on this issue. Will you carry on working or want your wife to carry on working? What are the advantages and disadvantages for:**
1 **the mother**
2 **the father**
3 **the children**

# 2 Marriage

The majority of men and women in Britain do get married. In the late 1970s between ninety and ninety-five per cent of people were married or had been married for a period by the time they were forty. If you asked a number of adults why they got married you might get many different answers. Some people might say it was because they were in love. They may not be able to explain what they meant by this though. Some might say that they wanted security. Some that they wanted to share their lives with somebody and have a companion. Others that they

wanted to extend an existing relationship. At some point however, most of these couples would say that having children was one of their reasons for getting married. Nine out of ten married couples have children of their own.

In some European countries in particular, there are people who choose to live together without getting married. Sometimes this is a temporary situation and the couple eventually get married. A survey in 1979 in Britain showed that twenty per cent of couples who married in the late 1970s had lived together before their marriage. In France in 1976 over forty per cent of couples had done this. There is also a proportion of people who live together all their lives and never marry.

The decision whether to get married or whether to form some sort of union or not is an important one. Sometimes people marry just to get away from their homes. This is often a mistake and can lead to further unhappiness. An unexpected pregnancy can also lead couples to marry. When this happens, families can exert a great deal of pressure on both partners to get married. The marriage could work out well, but there may be problems if the couple was forced into it. An unplanned pregnancy need not lead to marriage though. In Sweden about one third of all births are to unmarried couples.

---

**Imagine a conversation with your parents in which you tell them you have decided to live with your boyfriend or girlfriend rather than get married. Write down how you might persuade them that this was a good thing.**

**What do you think your parents might say?**

## Marriage patterns

In many countries, such as Britain, North America and Australia, a marriage is between one man and one woman. When the sociologist George Murdock studied 250 societies in different parts of the world in 1949, he found that less than fifty of the societies studied have this one man/one woman pattern. You must remember though that not all the 250 societies he studied were the same size, so that although one man/one woman is not the most usual marriage pattern in terms of numbers of societies, it is common to a large proportion of the world's population.

The one man/one woman marriage pattern is known as *monogamy*. *Mono* means one, *gamos* means marriage. *Bigamy* (*bi* meaning twice) occurs when a person marries for the second time while their first husband or wife is alive and they are not divorced. In Britain this is illegal. *Polygamy* (*poly* means many) is the custom of having many husbands or wives at the same time.

There are two kinds of polygamy. These are *polygyny* and *polyandry*. Polygyny is when one man has several wives. Polyandry is when one woman has several husbands.

### Polygyny

Polygyny is practised by the Tikhari tribe in the Cameroons in West Africa. The high chief or Fou may have as many as 150 wives. In this tribe there is a custom whereby the bridegroom gives the bride's parents gifts known as the brideprice. These gifts may be cattle, jewels or other goods. This practice means that only the wealthiest men can afford many wives. Therefore the more wives the chief has, the higher his status. Polygyny is also practised by some Muslim societies.

### Polyandry

The Khasa tribe in India practice polyandry. When a woman marries the eldest son in a family she must think of all his younger

A rich farmer in Ghana with his seven wives and some of their children.

brothers as her husbands as well. She is married to them all. All the men in the family accept equal responsibility for any children that are born. Polyandry is also customary in Tibet (see p. 6). Both polyandry and polygyny give rise to particular family patterns.

The type of marriage pattern found in a society is often related to the economy of that society. For example, where polygyny is practised a wife may have higher status by being married to a man who has several wives. As described above, the more wives a man has, the higher his status and the wealthier he needs to be. Therefore in poor societies, only the richer men will practise polygyny. The poorer men will have fewer women left available to marry. This could give rise to polyandry amongst the poorer people.

## Choosing a partner

As we have already seen, a large number of people do marry or stay with a partner for a long period in their lives. How do people choose who to spend their lives with? Some people in the world have their partners chosen for them, other choose their partner for themselves. Either way, there are a number of factors which influence that choice. Religion, age, nationality or race and class are among these factors.

### Religion

A recent survey in America showed that ninety-three per cent of Catholics marry Catholics. It also showed that ninety-seven per cent of Jews marry Jews. Although these percentages seem higher than one would expect, religion undoubtedly exerts a strong influence on choice of partners. For example, a young person who is sent to a Catholic or Jewish school will most likely have friends of the same religion.

### Age

Most couples are of similar ages. Usually the

man is the older partner. Of course there are exceptions to this.

### Nationality or race

With the improvement in communications all over the world, people of different nationalities and races are able to move and travel to different countries more easily. In cities, mixed-race marriages are increasing but they still form a small fraction of the total number

of marriages. People do tend to choose a long-term partner from their own ethnic group.

## Class

In Britain eighty-three per cent of people who marry tend to marry someone from the same social class or level of education. They are also more likely to marry someone from the same area.

---

**In a study of college students who were either engaged or recently married, it was found that eighty per cent of them had had an ideal partner in mind. What would your ideal partner be like? List the characteristics and attributes you would desire in a partner and rank them in order of importance. Is your list similar to your friends'? If it is, why do you think so? If not, why not?**

---

All over the world there are different methods of finding a partner. Customs and practices in different countries dictate who people marry. You will remember that during the past twenty years long-term stable unions without marriage have become far more common. It is also much more common nowadays than it was, to have only one parent bringing up children. In these cases a marriage may have failed and ended in divorce (see p. 25) or a partner may have died or have left.

When marriages do occur however, we can divide them into two sorts: those where people choose their partners for themselves, called *love marriages*, and those where the parents choose their son or daughter's partner, called *arranged marriages*.

## Love marriages

In societies where people choose their partners, age and class play a particularly influential role. People tend to choose friends of their own age and thus their partner. They will probably meet, go to school and work with people of the same class. This will influence who they choose as a partner. If a love marriage fails then the couple concerned must accept responsibility for the failure. Although family and friends may help, the burden is really on the couple themselves. If the couple marry for love it is hoped that they will want to spend the rest of their lives together.

---

**What do you think are the advantages of choosing your own partner? Are there any problems that you can think of? What do you think is a good age to get married? Why?**

---

## Arranged marriages

In parts of Africa and Asia it is the custom for marriages to be arranged by parents. When families have moved from these places to other countries where marriages are not arranged, they will often continue to practise this custom. In Britain today some upper-class parents still have a say in who their children marry.

When a marriage is arranged the boy and girl will meet and can say if they like each other. If all goes well, the couple become engaged. The engagement usually lasts for about a year. During this year the couple get to know each other and go out together. They may be accompanied by a relative or friend to stop any possible gossip about their behaviour. The couple will then marry.

There are many reasons why people think arranged marriages are a good idea. Firstly, the teenagers who are having their marriage arranged often think that their parents have more experience of life. With this experience they are more likely to choose the right person, with similar interests and of a similar background. Secondly, the teenagers feel there are more divorces in love marriages. If an arranged marriage does fail though, both sets of parents accept responsibility for the failure. The son or daughter often returns home into the family.

---

**This is what Geeta, a nineteen-year-old girl living in Britain, said about her**

mother who was trying to arrange a marriage for her.

'If my mum shows me a boy and I refuse, she does not mind. She asks me the reason and I tell her. If it is not my cup of tea I don't have it, and that's the case with most girls.' (From *Finding a Voice* by Amrit Wilson, Virago 1978.)

If your mum or dad was trying to arrange a marriage partner for you, what type of person would they choose? Ask your parents to give you a description of the type of person they think would suit you — and see if you agree with them! What other advantages can you see in having your marriage arranged?

Whether marriages are love marriages or arranged marriages it is often very difficult to find a partner, let alone an ideal partner. In societies where people marry who they choose, organisations have arisen that try to match people with others who are compatible. Sometimes this leads to firm relationships. Where marriages are arranged by the families there is at least security that a partner will be found. Marriage is something that needs to be worked at. Often love grows out of a marriage if both partners share the responsibility and contribute to it.

## The marriage contract

All societies have their own rules about marriage. This governs both the choice of partner and the ceremony itself. These rules fall into two areas. There is the legal side of marriage and the religious side of marriage.

### The legal contract

Many societies have laws governing marriage. For example in Britain, the couple must both be over sixteen. They must not be married already (any previous marriage must have been ended either by divorce or the death of one partner). In the Church of

A dating bureau advert.

England Prayer Book you will find a list of relations who cannot marry each other. For example, you cannot marry your brother or sister. This is against the law because of the dangers of what is known as *inbreeding*. Children born as a result of marriage between close blood relatives are more likely to suffer from either congenital defects or hereditary diseases (see p. 80). If any of these laws are broken the marriage is illegal. The couple could face prosecution.

The marriage ceremony itself is a legal contract. In Britain, the ceremony must be performed by a person authorised by the government. It is of course, up to the couple to choose whether they want to marry in a church or in a registry office. In the registry office the marriage is a civil ceremony and the authorised person is the registrar. Ministers of churches may apply to the government so that they may also legally marry people. If a minister or a religious leader has not been made an authorised person then the couple have to go through a civil ceremony as well as a religious one.

The law also states that the couple must appear before the registrar or minister. There they must swear in front of two or more witnesses that there is no reason why they should not marry. They have to promise they are old enough to marry, are not already married and are not closely related to each other, which is forbidden. Also they are required to post a notice of the marriage in

A registry office wedding.

some public place. This may be outside the registry office or in the church. For a church wedding the 'banns' may be called in the church. These are called by the vicar who asks three times, on different occasions, whether there is any reason why the couple should not be married.

In most states in North America, couples can marry in the street, in their sitting rooms or wherever they like. All that they have to do is to obtain a marriage licence and to ensure that a minister or judge is present to perform the ceremony.

## The religious contract

In the Christian Church, marriage is a life-long union. It is undertaken by a man and a woman for the producing and rearing of children. It is also for the help and companionship of the couple concerned. A ring symbolises that union. The handing over of the ring is an important part of the marriage service.

The religious service takes into account the legal contract, as we have just seen. In the religious ceremony the couple swear they will stay together 'till death us do part'. Some Christian churches recognise that marriages do not always last for ever. Although it is not possible to remarry in church it is possible to have a remarriage blessed by these churches. There are moves to allow people to remarry in church but as yet it is not allowed. The Roman Catholic Church does not recognise divorce at all and will not contemplate re-marriage unless the person concerned is a widow or widower.

An orthodox, which means strict, Hindu wedding is performed in the presence of the sacred fire. The marriage is completed after certain ceremonies, when the couple take seven steps together around the fire. A Hindu marriage is considered to be a sacred and in-dissoluble union between husband and wife. Divorce is therefore not recognised and the couple are bound to each other until death. In former times Hindu widows practised *sati*, which meant throwing themselves on the funeral pyres of their husbands to be burnt alive. They believed they were bound to their husbands after death as well as before. Hindus have a high view of marriage. Husbands and wives are called upon to adjust

A Hindu wedding ceremony.

their tastes, tempers, ideals and interests, instead of breaking up, when they find they differ. They seek to make marriage a success by means of compromise and adjustment.

In Islam, which is the religion of Muslims, marriage is said to be a contract which is signed by two guardians, one for each side of the marriage partnership. Under Islamic law a man may have up to four wives at one time. This is only provided that he can support and treat them all equally. In Britain and most other Western societies, only the first wife is recognised by civil law. Islam permits divorce and the actual process is quite easy. A Muslim husband only has to say 'I divorce you' three times. He need give no reason. This easy divorce procedure does not apply to women. However, there are certain grounds laid down in Islamic law whereby a woman can divorce her husband. For example, she could divorce him if he had failed to provide adequately for her for two years. Even though it is possible to be divorced in Islam, it is rare today.

---

**Perhaps some of your classmates have been to different types of weddings. Ask them to describe them and say what they liked or did not like about the particular service. Which type of wedding would you choose if you were getting married? Why?**

---

## Marriage and divorce

There has been a steady rise in divorce rates in industrial countries throughout this century. In 1911, 859 petitions for divorce were filed in England and Wales. In 1981 the figure was 170 000. The table below shows the divorce statistics in England and Wales from 1951 to 1981.

Sometimes the rising divorce rate is seen as a threat to stable family life. However many factors must be taken into account before people can say this. The population of Britain has more than doubled since the nineteenth century. A greater proportion of people marry now than did then. This means that there are more marriages than there were a hundred years ago and therefore a greater possibility of more marriages failing. An in-crease in *life expectancy*, which is the age to which people can reasonably expect to live, has meant that people are married for longer these days. Therefore marriages are exposed to greater risks of breakdown.

In 1857, in Britain, a divorce could only be obtained by a private Act of Parliament. Clearly, only the rich and powerful were in a position to end their marriages legally. Thus, the true rate of marriage breakdown was never known. The introduction of the Legal Aid Scheme in 1949 meant that more people could afford the cost involved in obtaining a divorce. The Divorce Law Reform Act, which came into effect in 1971, adopted a new approach to divorce. Under this law it is no longer necessary to find one partner guilty of adultery, cruelty or other offences for a divorce to be granted. The only reason

| England and Wales | 1951 | 1961 | 1971 | 1976 | 1977 | 1978 | 1979 | 1980 | 1981 |
|---|---|---|---|---|---|---|---|---|---|
| Petitions filed | 38 000 | 32 000 | 111 000 | 145 000 | 168 000 | 164 000 | 164 000 | 172 000 | 170 000 |
| Decrees absolute granted (divorces given) | 29 000 | 25 000 | 74 000 | 127 000 | 129 000 | 144 000 | 138 000 | 148 000 | 146 000 |
| Rate per thousand married population | 3 | 2.1 | 6.0 | 10.1 | 10.4 | 11.6 | 11.2 | 12.0 | 11.8 |

(From *Social Trends*, 1981)

necessary for divorce now is the 'irretrievable breakdown of marriage'. For the first time in our history, divorce can be obtained against the wishes of one of the partners, if the couple have lived apart for five years or more.

This has made divorce much easier and partly accounts for the dramatic increase in the divorce rate in 1971 (see table on p. 25). People who could not or would not file for divorce under the old law now did so. The increase in the divorce rate slowed down when the back-log of cases from the early 1970s had been cleared.

## Who gets divorced?

A study of divorce statistics does show that certain characteristics are associated with divorce. The age of the couple when they marry appears to be an important factor. Couples under the age of twenty when they marry are three times as likely to divorce. Young brides are also more often pregnant when they marry than older brides. This factor is associated with an increased risk of divorce too. Where couples marry someone of a different religion, class, race or nationality, there is again more risk of divorce. Perhaps this is because these marriages experience more pressure from friends and relatives. Divorce appears to be more common amongst couples who are childless. The most common length of marriage amongst divorced couples is four years. At present though, there is an increase in the number of divorces occurring in older couples who have been married for more than twenty years.

## For better or worse?

It is clear that there has been a change in attitude towards marriage. Perhaps Britain is less publicly religious than in the nineteenth century. The marriage vows of 'for better or worse' and 'till death us do part' have become weakened. Certainly there is less stigma attached to divorce nowadays. Some people believe that the greatest influence contributing towards the increasing

divorce rate is people's changing expectations of marriage. Nowadays, it is said, people expect more from marriage. They are not prepared to put up with a marriage without love and affection. Therefore they prefer to end the marriage and seek a new relationship elsewhere.

Certainly the increase in the divorce rate does not mean that marriage and the family have no future. Today divorce usually opens up the way for remarriage. Over one third of divorced people marry again within a year, showing that they still have faith in marriage. It must be remembered too, that we cannot really know the true extent of marriage breakdown in Britain. There will always be many more unhappy or broken marriages than ever reach the divorce courts.

## What about the children?

It is difficult to draw conclusions about the effect of divorce on children. It would be necessary to compare the problems experienced by children of divorced parents with those who have a disturbed family life. The happiness of these children is disrupted because their parents do not get on, but the parents do not get divorced. Clearly, most divorces do not just happen. There might have been months, even years of arguments and stress before the marriage broke up. Some experts believe that it is this which has a bad effect on children, rather than the divorce itself. Parents who stay together 'for the sake of the children' might be doing more harm than good. A stable, single-parent family is reckoned to be better for children than an arguing two-parent family.

Nevertheless, a five-year study of children from divorced families in California showed that divorce did hurt the children. They were shocked by the divorce and did not want their parents to do it. Younger children who cannot understand what is going on may blame themselves for the break-up. They may be frightened that their remaining parent will abandon them too. Many of the children had fantasies that their parents would get back together again. One of the problems

**How would you feel if you could only see your father by arrangement?**

seemed to be that few parents could talk to their children about what was happening. It appears that pre-school children and adolescents were the age-groups which had most difficulty in coming to terms with the divorce. However, reactions were widely different. Some children became more mature through this experience. So it seems that divorce can lead to disturbance or personal growth depending on a number of factors. These may be age, sex and the sort of stress that accompanied the divorce. The California study showed that it was most difficult for children in the first year after divorce if there was continued bitterness between the parents. Children want to remain on good terms with both their parents.

In Britain half the children of divorced parents lose contact with the parent who left within a few months. The law court has to determine who has *custody*, that is the right to look after the children, and how much *access* the other partner has, that is the right to see the children. Law courts are more likely to give the mother custody although in some cases the father now gets it. Sometimes the court orders one partner to pay *alimony*. This is either a regular payment from one partner to the other or a lump sum of money from one partner to the other. The court

determines how much money should be paid. It is more often the man who has to pay alimony although this is changing.

A growing, though still small number of conciliation bureaux are trying to help keep children in touch with both their parents. These bureaux try to safeguard the interests of the children and reduce the conflict between parents. Conciliators are usually fully qualified social workers with additional training in divorce law and court procedures. The conciliators mainly try to settle disputes about custody and access, but will also deal with property and financial settlements. The aim is to take the pressure off children, while putting their interests first.

**Write an article for a teenage magazine entitled 'Divorce is a necessary evil'. Try to explain to teenagers why so many of their parents' marriages might end in divorce. See if you can give some positive advice to enable them to cope if they should find themselves in this situation.**

*Divorce and stress*

The conciliation bureaux are trying to reduce the stress, particularly for the children, when a divorce occurs. When a person is continually subjected to demands that put their mental or physical energy under strain, they are said to be suffering from stress.

The factors that cause stress in one person may not cause stress in another person. Some people have a greater capacity to cope with stressful situations than others. Some situations that can cause stress are:

living in an environment where there are constant rows

the death of someone very close

the break-up of a marriage

constant ill health

poor living conditions

unemployment

loneliness

Can you think of other causes? Generally children and adults can cope with one of these aspects of stress without showing an obvious change in behaviour. However, if a child or adult is subjected to more than one kind of stress or the stressful situation persists, then their behaviour may change.

These are some of the symptoms of stress:

fidgeting
nail biting
stomach pains and sickness
skin problems
anxiety
depression
agitation
lack of concentration
muddled thinking

People react in different ways when under stress:

being silent and withdrawn from other people

preoccupation with other things

aggressive behaviour

illness can sometimes provide an escape from stress

Often the love, care and understanding of someone close, such as a wife, husband, mother or very close friend will help the adult or child to overcome their stress. Sometimes this is not adequate and medical help has to be sought. Generally teenagers and adults can talk about their problems and this helps to reduce the stress. In young children, who have not adequate language to express their feelings, the problem can be more difficult to treat. Young children can sometimes be observed 'playing out' their stress. Examples might be:

hitting a doll or teddy to release their anger

playing at doctors and nurses to release their fears

Can you think of other examples?

---

**Make a list of the people and situations in your life that cause stress for you. Discuss your list with those of your friends. Are they similar? How do you cope with stress in these situations? How do you react? Perhaps you could help each other to think of better ways of coping with the stress in your lives.**

---

# 3 Parents

If this advertisement appeared in your local paper it is unlikely that many people would apply for the job. Yet it is a description of a job that many people spend years of their adult life doing. It is the job of being a parent.

You might not have recognised this job-description, because we are encouraged to have a much more glamorous image of parents. How often have you seen in magazines or on the television an attractive, well-dressed, smiling mum beaming at her clean,

contented and angelic baby with good-looking and proud dad somewhere near by?

## The real responsibilities

This attractive image can be misleading. In reality the job is demanding and difficult as well as rewarding and fun. It is also very important. The first years of a child's life are often described as the most formative years. This means that during this time the child's body, mind and personality begin to be shaped for the future. Parents play a major role in this shaping. They influence their child's overall development in many different ways. A young baby is helpless and dependent, and will rely on her (or his) parents for survival. The parents are therefore responsible for the child's life and growth. This is called *physical development*. It is a very obvious responsibility, which most parents fully realise. The development of a child's body is only one aspect of development. Parents influence the development of their child's mind. This is called *intellectual development*. From birth, parents are the child's first and most important teachers.

Parents influence the way a baby thinks and feels about other people. This is the child's *social development*. The relationship a baby experiences with her parents is usually the beginning of this social development. Parents also influence the feelings a baby has about herself. This is called *emotional development*. The child experiences love and affection from her parents. This affects her emotional development.

A baby needs the help of her parents in order to develop physically, mentally, socially and emotionally. Each of these four areas of development is equally important. They all rely on parents recognising their child's needs. In order to achieve this, parents need to do a number of things.

1 They must observe the child's behaviour closely and thus get to know their baby well.

2 They must try to make their surroundings into a suitable *environment* in which the child can develop. This is explained further in Chapter 6.

3 They need to provide opportunities that will help to stimulate the child's development.

4 They need to give the child responsibility to help her grow and learn.

5 Parents must try to react in an appropriate way to the child's behaviour.

6 By trying to meet the child's needs parents can also help the growth of a baby's possible development or *potential*.

It is difficult to measure how successful parents have been or to say whether they are good or bad parents. If they have done their very best to meet their child's developmental needs, they can be called responsible parents. Having children requires a lot of thought and planning, both before and after the child is born.

## Making a responsible decision

All through their lives people make decisions. Some decisions are small, like deciding which colour shirt to wear when you get up in the morning. Other decisions are big, like deciding to change your job or to move house. The decision to become a parent is one which probably involves the greatest personal responsibility of all. It will bring about a noticeable change in life-style.

If the decision to have children is made hastily and without sufficient thought, it is very difficult to go back on it. The job of being a parent is not one where you can hand in your notice or be given the sack. Parents doing their job unwillingly tend to have negative attitudes. They are not only restricting their own lives but could be damaging the lives of their children. Even though this is such an important decision, some people do not think of it so much as a choice as the natural course of events. This attitude can lead to frustration later in life. It is most important therefore, that parents have chosen their new job, are committed to it and plan for it. This planning, preparation and commitment are all part of making a responsible decision.

## Preparation for the job

Very few new parents have any experience in the job they have just taken on. Although it is a demanding job which requires special knowledge and skills, no training or experience is necessarily available. Parents are expected to learn on the job. This can mean learning by mistakes. Most parents rely on what they remember of their own upbringing, advice from parents, friends, and the health visitor. They use their common sense and probably a child-care book. Is this good enough? Other jobs which involve responsibility for children — for example, teaching, nursery nursing and social work — require years of special training before work starts.

People have to discover the knowledge and skills required of responsible parents both before and after they decide to take on the job. Gradually more information and guidance is becoming readily available. This is in the form of books, magazines, television programmes, Open University courses, Health Education Council publicity, National Childbirth Trust courses and child development courses in schools.

## Commitment

For humans, the job of being a parent is an unusually long one. This is because human babies are particularly helpless when they are born and take many years to become adult. They are dependent on adults for a long period compared with most other mammals. The human task of parenthood therefore requires a long-term commitment and a lot of dedication.

This commitment should be discussed beforehand because it is essential that both partners should agree on the decision to have children.

If parents are fully aware of the nature of the job when they decide to have children,

they will have a positive attitude to their new responsibilities. They will expect and willingly accept the changes to their lives. This will enable them to enjoy to the full the rewards that being a parent can bring: a sense of achievement, a new experience, a challenge, a sense of being needed, the satisfaction of doing an important job to the best of your ability, the pleasure of sharing a task, experiencing new relationships, the pleasure of observing a child's development, the satisfaction of influencing the development of the next generation.

## Planned parenthood

We have already established that having children is a responsible task. People therefore need to control whether they have a family or not and when they have children. To do this they need to use a method of *birth control*. The use of birth control means that people can choose when to start their family, choose the number of children they want, and choose to space the births as they wish. This is in marked contrast to one hundred years ago when birth control was much more haphazard and some women produced a child every year. The main advantages of planning a family are:

1 A couple can have a family when they think they are ready, when they are old enough and have a stable relationship.

2 They can have children when they know they can provide for their needs — with adequate time, energy, knowledge and money.

3 They can space the children according to how demanding they find the job and to how many years they wish to spend bringing up children.

4 They can enjoy the challenge of parenthood at a time and a pace that suits them.

5 They can choose a time when the woman is healthy and strong and therefore in the best possible condition for a pregnancy.

This all sounds very easy and straightfor-

ward. Some may say it sounds cold and cal-
culating.

*Contraception* is a method of birth control
for planning a family with the advantages
listed above. It also means that the couple
can enjoy sexual intercourse as often as they
like without any fear of unwanted pregnancy.
Contraception is described in more detail on
page 38.

It would be unrealistic to think that all
couples follow a carefully thought-out plan
in having children. There are some people
who have problems with fertility and cannot
produce children as easily as they thought
they would. Others find parenthood different
from the way they anticipated it and change
their plans. Some find their situation
changes so that they can no longer provide
for as many children as they had originally
decided to have. Some people prefer not to
use contraceptives or cannot use them and
therefore cannot make such definite plans.
Contraceptives sometimes fail and force
people to change their plans. Some people
enter marriage or relationships without
thinking about the future.

It is impossible to say how many pregnancies are greeted with happiness and
excitement and how many are considered as
something that has to be coped with and
overcome. Most parents have a combination
of both feelings.

### When plans go wrong

In each of the situations below, there
is an unplanned pregnancy. Each one
presents problems for the couple
concerned. Each couple will be
shocked. What other feelings will they
have? They will need some time to
adjust and to discuss the future.
Suggest some positive steps each
couple can take to make the best of
their situation.

### Mark and Fiona

They have been going out together
since they were eighteen. They were
both living with their parents but
managed to see each other about three
or four evenings a week. At twenty
they got engaged, but thought they
ought to wait a couple of years before
getting married. However, after a year,
they became so fed up with travelling
between their parents' homes that they
decided to get married. On Mark's
twenty-first birthday they got married
and were lucky enough to get a council
flat. Both of them were keen to have
children, but as they had not been
working long and both were enjoying
their jobs, they decided to start a
family in their mid-twenties. However,
six months after their wedding, Fiona
discovers that she is pregnant.

### Linda and Dave

They are in their forties. They married
young and had a family quickly. Their
daughter Sonia, now twenty, has
moved to Liverpool where she is living
in a bedsit and training to be a nurse.
Paul their son, who is eighteen, is in
the army and away from home most of
the time.

When their children moved away,
Linda and Dave found the house very
quiet and empty for the first time in
twenty years. Their new freedom came
as quite a shock. However, they
gradually adjusted and Linda got
herself a job. She enjoyed the new
friends she made and the extra money
was very useful. Linda and Dave
started going out more and enjoying
holidays abroad.

At forty-four, Linda is amazed to
discover that what she thought was the
beginnings of the menopause (see p. 34),
is in fact the third month of a
pregnancy.

### Angela and Ian

Sixteen-year-old Angela lives with her
parents and has a job as a secretary.
She has a steady boyfriend, Ian, who is
training to be a car mechanic. They

have recently been on holiday together, camping in Cornwall. While on holiday Angela and Ian had sexual intercourse for the first time. After they have been home a month Angela finds that she is pregnant.

## The beginnings of life

Parental responsibility really begins at the moment of *conception*. Conception is when the sex cells of the mother and father join together to create the beginning of a new human life. To understand exactly what happens, we need to know more about the two cells involved.

*The mother's sex cell*

Inside a woman's body there are two *ovaries*. Each ovary contains hundreds of thousands of tiny immature egg cells. These have been there since before the woman was born. These egg cells are the female sex cells. They are sometimes called *ova* (singular *ovum*). From puberty until middle age, the pituitary gland near the woman's brain produces hormones every month. These hormones stimulate the egg cells in her ovaries to mature. After about two weeks one egg cell which has ripened more than the rest is released from the ovary and drawn into the end of a tube leading out of the ovary. This is called the *fallopian tube*. The process is called *ovulation* and it occurs on average every four weeks.

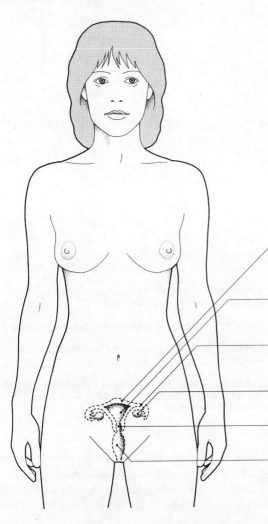

Female reproductive organs.

**Placenta.** The placenta or afterbirth grows on the lining of the uterus during pregnancy. It is a spongy mass of blood vessels linked to the baby by the umbilical cord. Its main job is to protect and nourish the baby.

**Uterus.** This is the medical name for the womb. Normally the size of a pear, it gets much bigger during pregnancy because this is where the baby grows.

**Fallopian tube.** This is the tube along which the eggs travel from the ovary to the uterus. There is one leading from each ovary and they are about four inches long.

**Ovary.** The ovary is the egg store. One tiny egg is released each month.

**Cervix.** The cervix is the neck of the uterus. It is the tiny entrance to the uterus which is capable of stretching during birth.

**Vagina.** The vagina is the birth canal. It is a passage about four inches long leading from the cervix to the opening between the legs. (The walls of the vagina are very elastic and it adjusts to the penis during sexual intercourse, as well as to the baby's head and shoulders during delivery.)

Each egg cell is about the size of a full stop. Under a microscope a central nucleus can be seen easily. The ripened egg cell then begins its journey down the fallopian tube and into the *uterus*. At the same time as ovulation, hormones from the ovaries cause the lining of the uterus to become thicker and richer. If the egg cell is fertilised by a male sex cell, it will be able to nestle into the nourishing lining of the uterus and grow.

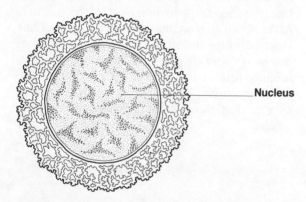

The female sex cell or egg.

However, if the egg cell is not fertilised, it breaks down and the lining of the uterus shrinks and separates from the wall of the uterus. The unfertilised egg cell, together with the lining and a small amount of blood are then pushed out of the uterus through the cervix and into the vagina. A period or *menstruation* begins. At the same time, the pituitary gland stimulates the ovaries to ripen some more eggs ready to start the next cycle. This 28-day routine is called the menstrual cycle. In some women, particularly young women, menstruation does not occur every twenty-eight days and periods are more irregular. During middle age, at about the age of forty-five, this whole process stops and the ovulation no longer takes place. This is called the *menopause*. It denotes the end of a woman's ability to have children. She is no longer fertile.

### The father's sex cell

The male sex cells, called *sperm*, are produced in the testicles. Normal body tempera-ture is a couple of degrees too high for the production of sperm. The testicles are there-fore situated in the scrotum, which hangs outside a man's body at a lower temperature than the rest of him.

During puberty the pituitary gland starts to cause the testicles to produce a steady supply of sperm. This supply continues until old age. Men are therefore fertile throughout their life. The penis is connected to the scrotum. The sperm pass out of the body, through the end of the penis.

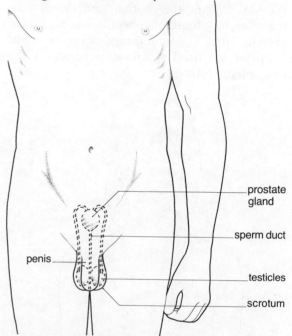

**Scrotum.** This is a sack of skin which contains the testicles. It is directly under the base of the penis.

**Testicles.** These are responsible for producing the male sperm.

**Prostate gland.** This produces the seminal fluid which mixes with the sperm.

**Sperm duct.** The sperm travel from the testicles, pass the prostate gland to the opening at the end of the penis in a tube called the sperm duct.

Male reproductive organs.

Each tiny sperm cell consists of a head, middle piece and tail. Each one is so small that it is invisible to the naked eye. It has been calculated that the number of sperm

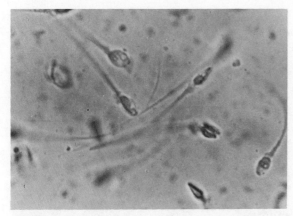

Motile human sperm.

equal to the present population of the earth would easily fit into a thimble. The sperm pass out of a man's body in a whitish liquid called seminal fluid. This is a nutritious fluid in which the sperm can swim.

## Fertilisation

Amongst living things there are various methods of joining a male and a female sex cell together, to fertilise and make a new life. In humans the ideal conditions for fertilisation are found in the fallopian tube of the mother. This means that the father's sperm must enter the mother's body. This happens during sexual intercourse. When a man is sexually aroused, his penis becomes stiff and erect and a perfect shape to fit into a woman's vagina. When a woman is sexually aroused, she produces a lubricant in her vagina. During intercourse the man pushes his penis into the vagina. The lubricants in the vagina aid this process. As the couple continues to make love both parties may approach a sexual climax. At the climax of the man's sexual excitement (*orgasm*), small amounts of seminal fluid containing a hundred to four hundred million sperm are discharged from the end of the penis and left in the vagina. This is called *ejaculation*.

The sperm then travel through the cervix, into the uterus and then into the fallopian tubes. This journey takes about six hours.

The shape of the sperm is carefully designed for this journey. They swim, head first, propelled by the tail and supplied with energy from the middle section, and nourishment from the seminal fluid.

If the sperm, while swimming along the fallopian tube, meet an egg cell, they eagerly cluster around it. The first sperm to touch the outer wall of the egg cell is readily accepted by it. Its head penetrates into the surface. At the same time, the egg cell wall hardens which prevents any more sperm getting in. Once the head of the sperm has joined with the nucleus of the egg cell, the middle section and tail of the sperm separate from the head and are destroyed. The cells of the future parents have met for the first time. The egg cell has been fertilised by the sperm. This is the moment of conception.

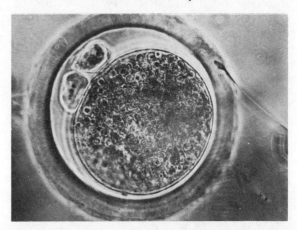

Sperm penetrating the surface of the ovum, as seen under the electron microscope.

Although the sperm are readily available in a man's body, there is only a short time in each menstrual cycle when the female is ready to conceive. The single egg cell which is released each month only lives for twelve to twenty-four hours before it breaks up. Most sperm live for about thirty-six hours before they die, and six of these hours are spent travelling up to the fallopian tube. Therefore the best time for intercourse to occur to ensure conception is probably the day before ovulation. At this time, a small plug of mucus (a thick jelly-like substance), which is always present in the cervix, becomes more runny so that sperm can swim more easily through it. Also, the lining of the uterus thickens ready to receive the fertilised egg. The woman's body is ready for conception to take place and during this short time, she is fertile. However, she will probably be unaware of these changes. The only outward indication is a slight increase in her body temperature which occurs during ovulation.

*Twins*

Sometimes two separate egg cells are re-leased from the ovaries and are fertilised by two different sperm. Both fertilised eggs are separate and have originated from different cells. They will become two people who are not particularly alike. These are called *fraternal* or non-identical twins. Twins of different sexes are always fraternal twins. Sometimes, when one egg cell has been fertilised by one sperm, for some reason the fertilised cell splits into two. Two identical babies develop together. These are called *identical* twins.

## Passing on family likeness

The sex cells from each parent that join together to create the beginning of a new life, are unique to that couple. Contained in each sperm and egg cell is 'information' which is essential to the development of the new in-dividual. The information 'programmes' the order in which development will take place and the details of what the new person is going to be like. Although the combined sperm and egg cells produce a completely unique person (an individual), in some ways we are all like our parents or other members of our families because we inherit infor-mation from them.

In order to understand this more precisely, we must look at the sex cells in greater detail. In the nucleus of each of the sperm and the egg cells are the basic units of information called *genes*. These are so tiny that they are difficult to see using the most powerful

Family likeness.

microscope. However, we do know that the genes are linked together into *chromosomes*. They are like beads threaded on a necklace. Each chromosome has hundreds of thousands of genes.

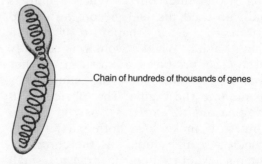

Chain of hundreds of thousands of genes

A chromosome.

With the exception of the sex cells, every single cell in our bodies is made up of twenty-two pairs of identical chromosomes plus two other chromosomes. The twenty-two pairs control our body appearance and functions. The other two chromosomes determine our sex. These sex chromosomes can be easily identified because of their shape. One is shaped like a Y and is called the *Y chromosome*. The other one is shaped like an X and is called the *X chromosome*. All females have two X chromosomes, giving them feminine characteristics. All males have one X and one Y chromosome, giving them male characteristics.

## Boy or girl

The sperm and the egg are different from the other body cells. They are made up of twenty-three single chromosomes. After fertilisation, the twenty-three egg cell chromosomes pair up with the twenty-three sperm chromosomes. These form the new cells which gradually multiply and develop to form the *embryo* (see p. 47). Each sex cell only contains one chromosome which determines sex. In the female egg cell it is always an X chromosome. The father produces two types of sperm cells though. Some sperm cells

contain an X and some a Y. If an X chromosome from the father fertilises with the X chromosome of the mother's egg, the resulting baby will be a girl. If a Y chromosome from the father fertilises with the X chromosome of the mother's egg, the baby will be a boy. Hence, the father's sperm decides the sex of the child. Each time an egg is fertilised, there is an equal chance of the baby being a boy or a girl.

The sex of the new individual is only one piece of information contained in the genes of the fertilised cells. The other twenty-two chromosomes supply information for body appearance, abilities and temperament. Together these details or characteristics make up someone who is different from anyone else in the world. In the case of identical twins, however, identical information is inherited. This is because both twins originated from the same sperm and egg cells which later split. As a result two identical people are created (see p. 36).

Genes

Egg containing 22 body
chromosomes plus one X

Sperm containing 22 body
chromosomes plus one X *or* one Y

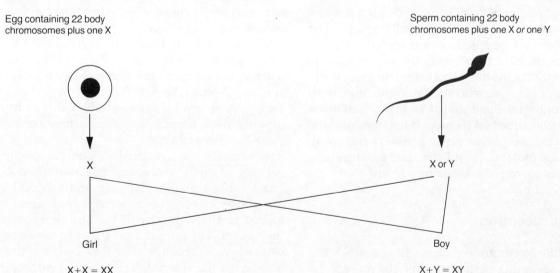

X

X or Y

Girl

Boy

X+X = XX

X+Y = XY

## The influence of the environment

It is obvious that characteristics such as hair and eye colour, shape of nose or size of head

are directly a result of the information in our genes. However, it is important to realise that some of the information can be strongly

influenced by our *environment* (our surroundings). This means that our genes and
the environment together determine what we
are like. Some things, however, are thought
to be determined solely by the environment
we are in.

What exactly is meant by our environment,
which seems to play such an important part
in the sort of people we become? It consists
of everything and everyone we come into
contact with throughout our lives: our surroundings at home, at school, on holiday, at
work and when we go out. Our parents, relations, teachers, friends, workmates are all
parts of our environment. The climate we live
in, the diseases we catch are all our environment. What will happen to the boy who has
inherited the ability to do well at school but
whose parents and teachers do not encourage
him to work hard? What will happen to the
girl who has genes for a large body build, but
who has not been given an adequate diet?
What will happen to the girl who has inherited the ability to swim well, but has
never been taken to a swimming pool or the
seaside?

Many inherited abilities need opportunities
and encouragement to develop fully. For
many years, people have expressed different
opinions about the importance of genetic
inheritance (nature) and the influence of the
environment (nurture). We know that both
are important and that it is difficult to put a
value on either on its own. It appears that the
information in our genes presents the possibilities (potential) and that our environment
makes them possible or impossible.

# Contraception

Sexual intercourse (*coitus*) is necessary for
the beginning of a new life. However, it is
also a very pleasurable experience. A couple
may want to express their love for each
other, without producing children.

In order to enjoy sexual intercourse without producing children, one or both of the
partners can use a *contraceptive. Conception*
means becoming pregnant and *contra* means
against. *Contraception* means the prevention of fertilisation and pregnancy. As
you have already seen it is often called birth
control. There are many contraceptive
methods available today which prevent the
male sperm joining the female egg cell during
sexual intercourse.

*Early methods of preventing pregnancy*

For many years, in most countries, people
were encouraged to have large families. It
was necessary to have a lot of children to
maintain the family workforce. In addition,
disease, famine and great hardship caused
the early death of many children.

Despite this, there are records to show that
people were concerned about preventing pregnancy as far back as five thousand years
ago. Because there was very little understanding of how fertilisation takes place, the
early methods in primitive societies were
based on folklore and superstition. The
Chinese, for instance, probably originated
the idea that if the woman held her breath
and thought of other things at the moment of
her partner's ejaculation, then conception
would not take place. In medieval France,
any woman who did not wish to conceive was
told to cut off the foot of a female weasel and
wear it around her neck during sexual intercourse. Women in Siberia used to believe
they could avoid conception simply by
dipping their fingers into the bath water of
their firstborn child.

As time went on, methods of contraception
became a little more logical, though not
much more reliable. Ear wax and crocodile
dung were just two of the strange ingredients
placed in the vagina with the aim of killing
the sperm. The only reason these sometimes
worked was because they blocked off the
passage of the sperm to the uterus. Feathers,
seed pods and leaves were also used as a
barrier. Pieces of animal intestines stitched
at one end were used as a primitive sheath
over the penis to prevent sperm being left in
the vagina. At one time, the flushing out or
douching of the vagina after intercourse was

very popular. Oil, vinegar and baking soda were some of the substances recommended for this.

*A serious need for birth control*

It was not until the late eighteenth century that there seemed to be a more serious need for reliable methods of preventing conception. It was at this time that some people became concerned about the possible effects of the increasing birth rate. In 1798 Dr Malthus, an economist and clergyman, predicted a 'population explosion'. People suggested that contraception was the only answer to this problem. However, this idea was met with horror and disapproval, for never before had such matters been discussed openly. They were considered sordid and shameful. During the nineteenth century the population continued to rise and poverty and overcrowding increased, particularly in industrial towns.

*Changing attitudes*

The widespread opposition to birth control could not be changed quickly. People who made and sold contraceptives had to operate in secret. The view commonly held was that sexual intercourse was only for producing children and that more self-control in sexual matters was needed to reduce the population. This idea was strongly backed by most people connected with the Church. They felt then, that God was part of the process of creating children. Many people from the medical profession were also against any sort of interference with sexual intercourse because of the dangers to health. At the end of the nineteenth century, the British government supported the ideas of the Church and the medical profession, and a number of anti-contraceptive laws were passed. Anybody promoting birth control could then be prosecuted in the courts.

Those who wished to change these ideas had two main reasons. One was the view put forward by Dr Malthus — the effect of the increasing population on the economy of the country. They could foresee major problems in housing, employment, health and food supplies. The other view was an idea promoted by a lady called Marie Stopes who considered that sexual intercourse was a natural part of any marriage relationship. She was concerned about the strain on husbands and wives who were trying to avoid having children by limiting sexual intercourse.

Despite enormous opposition, contraception continued to be promoted through public meetings, pamphlets and books. The government was pressurised and clinics offering contraception to married women were opened under the guise of child welfare clinics. Very gradually, over the past sixty years, more and more people have recognised the need for birth control. Eventually, the government had to take some notice. Slowly, laws have become more liberal so that the clinics started by the Family Planning Association in Britain in the 1930s are now part of the National Health scheme, financed by the government. They offer a completely free service, giving contraceptive advice on techniques to men and women. During the last twenty years, the need for birth control for unmarried people has also been recognised. In 1963 the first Brook Advisory Centre was opened, offering contraceptive advice to single people. Brook Centres are now also partly financed by the government.

## Better methods of contraception

Greater acceptance of the need for birth control made it easier for doctors and scientists to develop more reliable methods of contraception than were available a hundred years ago. A greater understanding of fertilisation has enabled a range of scientifically based and safer contraceptives to be obtained today.

On the following pages, there is a description of all the main methods and a chart summarising the characteristics of each.

All of these can be obtained free in Britain from a family doctor or health centre, a

Family Planning Association clinic or Brook Advisory Centre. Married and single people of both sexes can be advised and supplied with contraceptives as long as they are over sixteen years of age. Brook Centres will also advise girls under the age of sixteen.

## The pill

The pill or oral contraceptive contains the hormones *oestrogen* and *progestogen*. These are synthesised versions of the hormones oestrogen and progesterone which occur naturally in the body. The effect these hormones have on a woman's body is to prevent ovulation occurring. In other words, the hormones prevent the female egg being released and therefore there is no possibility of fertilisation taking place. Another effect the hormones prevent the eggs from being the mucus plug in the cervix, making it much more difficult for the sperm to get through to the uterus.

The pill containing the two hormones is called the combined pill and the woman usually takes it for twenty-one days. During

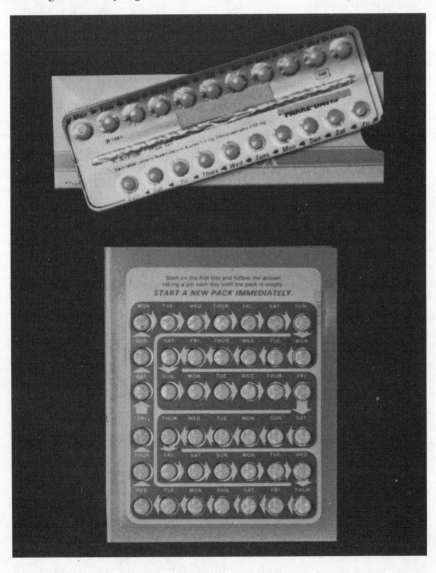

the following seven days no pill is taken During this week, a period usually occurs. The woman then starts her twenty-one day cycle again. Every pack of pills is specially designed to make it easy to take them according to plan.

The pill has only been prescribed in Britain since 1960. Because it is fairly new, doctors are still not absolutely sure of its long-term effects.

### The progestogen-only pill

There is also a pill which contains only progestogen. This is sometimes called the mini-pill. This thickens the mucus plug in the cervix but does not stop ovulation. This pill is usually taken continuously. It is less reliable than the combined pill.

### The intra-uterine device
(IUD, sometimes called the coil or loop)

An IUD is a small, flat, flexible object made of plastic and sometimes wound with copper. It fits just inside the uterus. The IUD works partly by preventing the fertilised egg from settling in the lining of the uterus. Various types of IUD are used in Britain. Some are more suited to women who have not had

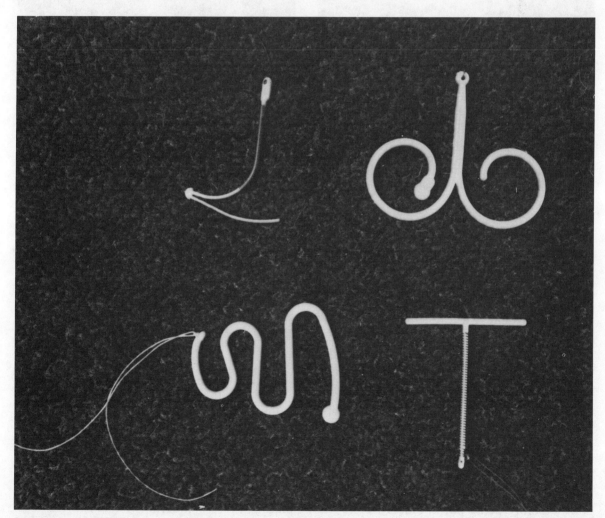

Intra-uterine devices.

children. Others are more suited to those who have. Once it has been fitted, the IUD requires no attention, unless it is wound with copper, when it needs renewing every two to three years.

## The cap or diaphragm

The cap is soft rubber dome mounted on a pliable metal ring. A woman puts it into her vagina so that it fits over her cervix (entrance to the uterus). It is usually put in place before sexual intercourse and left there for at least six hours afterwards. The cap forms a barrier which prevents sperm from getting into the uterus to fertilise the egg. For added protection the cap is also smeared with a cream or foam which kills sperm — a *spermicide* — before being put in place.

## The sheath
(condom, French letter, protective, male contraceptive)

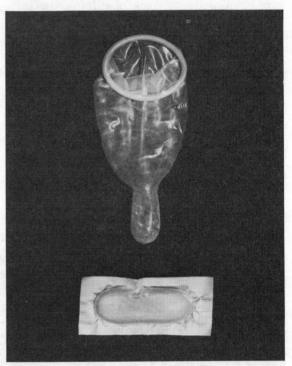

Sheaths are made of thin rubber, and are worn over the penis during sexual intercourse. They prevent sperm from entering the vagina and therefore prevent fertilisation. The sperm and semen which come out of the penis during ejaculation are trapped in the closed end of the sheath. The sheath should be rolled onto the penis after it has become hard and erect.

For extra protection, the woman is advised to use spermicides. These are creams or foams that kill sperm. The spermicide should be placed in the vagina before intercourse. This gives some protection should any sperm spill from the sheath or if it should split. After intercourse, the man should hold the sheath firmly in place until after withdrawal. Sheaths are easy to obtain and can be bought from barbers, chemists, clinics, or by mail order. One additional advantage of using the sheath is that it protects both partners from passing on any infections.

*Sterilisation*

Sterilisation is a permanent method of birth control which involves an operation for a man or woman.

It is an ideal method for couples who have completed their family or who know *for sure* that they don't want any more children.

*Female sterilisation* consists of the fallopian tubes being closed so that the egg cannot travel down to meet the sperm and be fertilised. The operation is done under a general anaesthetic.

*Male sterilisation* is done by blocking off the tubes through which the sperm travel from the testicles to the penis. This means that no sperm are released from the penis during ejaculation. The operation is minor and is done under local anaesthetic.

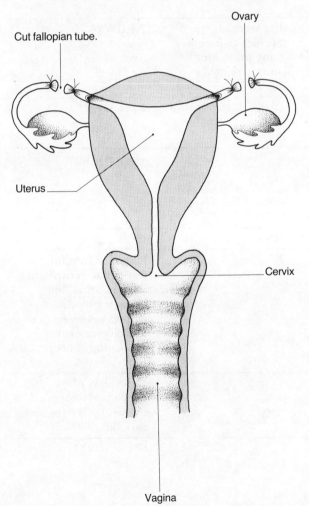

Female sterilisation.

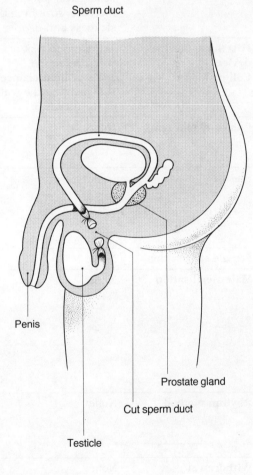

Male sterilisation.

The following table compares the various methods of contraception and there advantages and disadvantages with regard to such factors as the risks to health and reliability.

| Name | Health risks | Reversibility | Reliability |
|---|---|---|---|
| **The combined pill** | 1 Slight risk of blood clots, particularly in diabetics, cigarette smokers, women with high blood pressure, or with a history of heart attacks in family. The risk increases for a woman over 35. 2 Some women suffer side effects, e.g. headaches, weight increase, sore breasts, sickness and depression | √ | 100% if the instructions are followed. Occasionally vomiting and diarrhoea prevent the pill being absorbed by the body. |
| **IUD (intra-uterine device) Coil or loop** | 1 Increased risk of pelvic infection 2 Very slight chance of IUD piercing the wall of the uterus | If a woman decides to have a baby the doctor simply removes the IUD | 2-4 HWY* |
| **Cap or diaphragm** | None | √ | 3 per HWY* |
| **Sheath** | None | √ | 4 per HWY* |
| **Female sterilisation** | None | X | 100% |
| **Male sterilisation** | None | X | It is very rare for fertility to return after the operation, but occasionally the pathway does reopen. The chance of this happening is about 1 in 1000 |
| **Rhythm method** | None | √ | 47 per HWY* Very unreliable for women with irregular periods |
| **Withdrawal** | None | √ | 17 per HWY* |

* HWY means that of 100 women using this method, the number stated will become pregnant each year, e.g. 17 per HWY means that 17 out of each 100 women using this will become pregnant each year.

| Interference with intercourse | Effective straight away? | Medical examination required | Effect on periods |
|---|---|---|---|
| None | Not for the first 14 days of the first pack | √ | 1 Relieves pain<br>2 Reduces bleeding<br>3 Makes periods more regular<br>4 Relieves pre-menstrual tension |
| None | Yes | √ | Periods are often heavier than normal |
| The woman has to remember to put the cap in place beforehand | Yes | √ | None |
| 1 Putting sheath on erect penis interrupts love making<br>2 Slightly reduces sensitivity for men | Yes | X | None |
| None | Yes | √ | None |
| None | Not until tests prove that there are no sperm left in the tubes | √ | None |
| Prevents intercourse for part of every month | | X | None |
| 1 Intercourse must stop before the man's climax<br>2 The woman is unlikely to be relaxed<br>3 Can cause frustration to both partners | | X | None |

*The rhythm method or safe period*

This method of contraception requires no mechanical aids but relies entirely on avoiding sexual intercourse a few days before and after ovulation. This is when the woman is most fertile. It you look back to the section on fertilisation, you will remember that ovulation comes roughly midway between periods, but is difficult to detect. As a rough guide, women with a twenty-eight day cycle should avoid intercourse from the seventh to the eighteenth day. The remainder can be regarded as the safe period.

There are three ways a woman can try to find out when ovulation occurs

1 Taking her temperature daily and noting the slight drop in temperature at the time of ovulation followed by a slight rise immediately afterwards. This is called the temperature method.

2 Noticing the change in the mucus plug in the cervix which occurs about four days before ovulation. She will notice a clear, jelly-like discharge from the vagina or experience a sensation of wetness. This is called the Billings method.

3 Keeping a close record of her periods over a number of months to try to work out when ovulation takes place and therefore know her safe period in advance. This is called the calendar method.

Some people combine two or three of these in an attempt to be as safe as possible. However, this is a very unreliable method. Working out the time of ovulation is very difficult anyway and is even harder for women with irregular periods. Even if the dates are worked out correctly the woman may still become pregnant.

The rhythm method may be the only acceptable method for some couples whose religious or personal beliefs prevent them from using other methods of contraception. This method requires careful observation and record-keeping and a lot of will power.

*Withdrawal*

The medical name for this is *coitus interruptus*. It involves the man withdrawing his penis from the woman's vagina just before reaching a climax. In this way, the sperm are ejaculated outside the woman's vagina. It is a very unreliable method of contraception. Live sperm may be released before ejaculation without the man knowing.

## Making decisions

Despite the dramatic change in the general attitude and availability of methods of birth control during this century, there is still a wide range of opinions today. Many people still strongly disapprove of sexual intercourse outside marriage. In some families, contraception is not openly talked about. It is therefore possible that people do not know much about the various techniques and are embarrassed to find out about them. Many people do not use certain methods for religious reasons. Some continue to find the whole idea distasteful and unnatural.

Couples have to consider the advantages and disadvantages of the methods available. After discussion and advice, they will then make a decision which best suits them. No contraceptive will be effective unless the couple has planned to use it. Unwanted pregnancies can be avoided with responsible planning and forethought.

As yet there is no such thing as an ideal contraceptive. That is one which reliably prevents conception without causing any health risks, without affecting sexual intercourse in any way and which is reversible. Research is still continuing to try to find better techniques. In future years, there may be more convenient and reliable methods of contraception, which are acceptable to more people.

# The early development of the fertilised egg

*Day 1* About twenty-four hours after the egg cell has been released from the ovary, it meets the sperm swimming up the fallopian tube. One sperm manages to penetrate the wall of the egg cell. The sperm and egg cell fuse to make a fertilised egg.

*Days 2-3* The muscles in the wall of the fallopian tube cause the fertilised egg to be gently carried along towards the uterus. The egg begins to divide and subdivide, to make a solid cluster of cells. It is provided with food and oxygen by a fluid produced in the tube.

This fluid and the muscles in the wall of the fallopian tube are controlled by hormones produced by the ovaries.

*Days 4-6* The ball of cells reaches the end of the tube and enters the uterus. It is called an *embryo*. A thick heavy lining has formed on the walls of the uterus. The embryo now consists of about 64 cells.

*Day 7* The embryo (no larger than a pinhead at this stage) sticks on to the lining of the uterus. Here it will obtain shelter and nourishment. This is called implantation.

The woman's period will now be due, but of course, she will not have one.

The journey of the fertilised egg in its first 7 days.

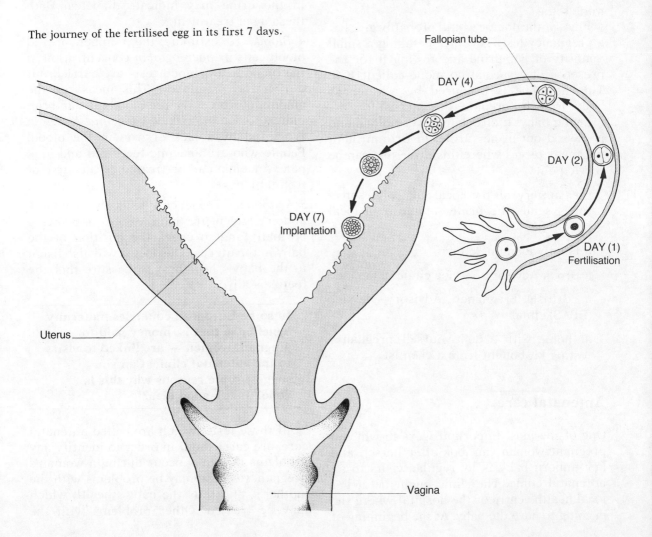

## Pregnancy testing

Once a woman misses a period and thinks she is pregnant, she is usually very keen to get it confirmed. If she goes to her doctor, he or she will probably ask her if she has missed a period and if her breasts feel tender. The doctor will also want to know if she has had any sickness and if she has been passing water more frequently than usual. These are all signs of pregnancy.

The doctor will then examine her heart, breasts and abdomen to get an idea of her general health. He or she will also feel her uterus, where the baby will grow. As you might expect, if she is pregnant the uterus will get bigger. This is called a pelvic examination.

Finally, the doctor would probably give her a pregnancy test. This means taking a small quantity of her urine and testing it for the presence of a special hormone called HCG. This hormone is produced by a woman's body to help prepare the uterus for the growing baby. It circulates in her blood and is passed out in her urine. In Britain there are many places where this urine test can be carried out:

the surgery of the local GP (who sometimes sends the urine sample to a local hospital)

a Family Planning clinic

a Brook Advisory Service clinic

a British Pregnancy Advisory Service (BPAS) clinic

at home with a do-it-yourself pregnancy testing kit bought from a chemist

## Antenatal care

One of the most important ways in which a pregnant woman can look after herself and her unborn baby is by regular visits to an antenatal clinic. The clinic might be at her local health centre or the hospital where she is going to have the baby. At the beginning of pregnancy, visits are only necessary every six to eight weeks. As pregnancy progresses visits become more frequent. In the final month before the birth weekly visits are necessary. Many women alternate visits to the hospital with visits to their local GP or midwife. This is called shared care.

This is what the doctor or midwife will check at a routine antenatal visit:

*1 Weight*   A careful record is kept to ensure that she is not gaining too much weight.

*2 Blood pressure*   Increased blood pressure can lead to the condition called *toxaemia.*

*3 Urine*   Protein found in the urine may also indicate toxaemia (see p. 57). Sugar present in the urine may indicate diabetes. Both these need treatment.

*4 Blood*   To estimate the number of red blood cells or *haemoglobin* concentration in the blood a few blood tests are carried out during the pregnancy. This measures the amount of iron in the red blood cells and can indicate a condition called *anaemia.* Anaemia is caused by a lack of iron in the blood. People who are anaemic feel tired and look pale. Anaemia can be treated by a course of iron tablets.

*5 Abdomen*   The doctor feels the woman's abdomen to ensure that the foetus is growing normally and to check the position of the baby in the uterus. The doctor will also listen to the baby's heartbeat to be sure that the foetus is alive.

---

**In some European countries maternity benefits — that is, money paid to pregnant women — are linked to visits to the antenatal clinic. Can you suggest some reasons why this is done? Is it a good idea?**

---

All these tests, which are called antenatal care, are carried out in order to identify any problems that may occur during a woman's pregnancy. These may be problems with the mother's, and thus the baby's health which may be treated. Other problems with the

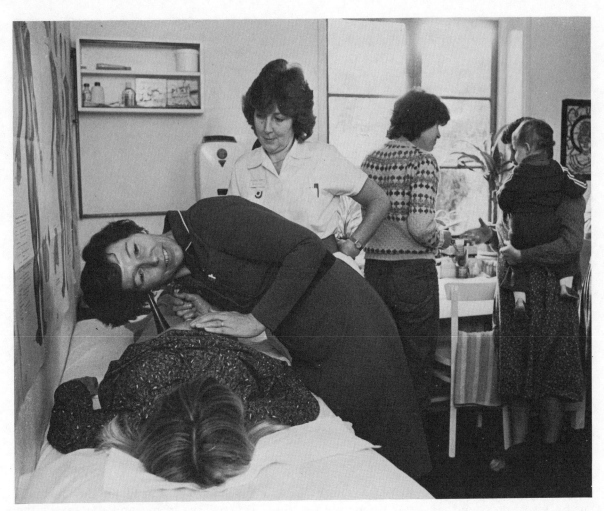

An Antenatal clinic.

baby which are more difficult to spot can still be detected from more detailed tests. The defects which need to be spotted are called *congenital defects*. This means that the disorder is present within the child and is present at the birth of the child.

## Recognising abnormalities in early pregnancy

All congenital disorders in a child are present at birth. Even so they may not show until the child is several years old, e.g. haemophilia.

If serious defects can be detected early enough in pregnancy the mother can be offered the opportunity of an abortion (see p. 59). Sometimes the human body will abort a seriously abnormal foetus naturally. In this case the mother has a miscarriage. Miscarriages do not only occur when the baby is abnormal though. Many women miscarry for other reasons, e.g. a bad fall (see p. 65). In these cases the baby may be quite normal. Some women who are carrying an abnormal foetus will not wish to have an abortion. They will have the baby as they planned. As with all decisions throughout the whole of pregnancy and childbirth, the decision is one that needs to be taken by the couple concerned.

There are three ways of detecting defects before birth.

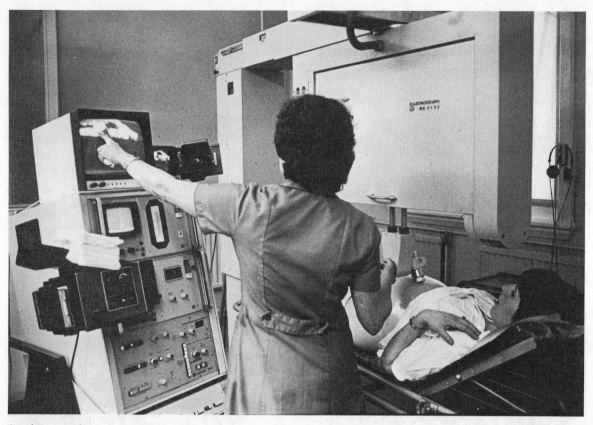

An ultra-sound scan.

### Ultra-sound scans

In this method, a picture of the baby is built up by directing sound waves at the baby in the uterus. The sound waves reflect a picture on a screen, showing any hard matter, e.g. bone. These scans help to detect any abnormalities in the formation of the head and spine. Many women will have at least one scan at some time in their pregnancy in Britain.

### Amnioscentesis

The unborn baby floats in the uterus in a fluid called *amniotic fluid*. This test involves taking a small sample of this fluid and testing it. A fine needle is put through the wall of the mother's stomach and a small sample of the fluid is removed. Various tests on the fluid will show if the baby has spina bifida or serious brain defects, which would probably cause death before or at birth. The tests will show Downs' syndrome and the sex of the baby. The latter could be important with genetic abnormalities which are passed only to the male sex, e.g. haemophilia. Amnioscentesis is done far less often than it used to be because ultra-sound scans are used instead.

### Family history examination

During pregnancy and sometimes even before conception, doctors discuss with parents their family history. The doctor will try to establish any abnormalities in the family and try to gauge the likelihood of the defect occurring again. Sometimes the parents will have to have blood tests. Future babies who may have Rhesus problems may be identified by this.

# 4 Pregnancy

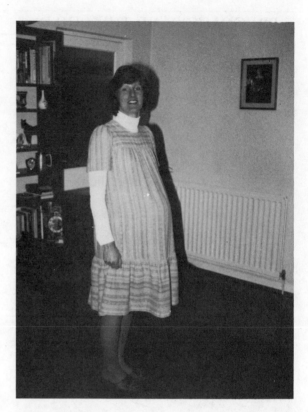

## How does it feel to be pregnant?

These are the feelings experienced by one new mother in the early months of her pregnancy.

'I was so anxious to know if I was pregnant that I had the test done by the chemist. Returning home my expression was enough to tell my husband it was positive and we hugged each other for joy. Weeks later I still felt like shouting it out as I walked along the road. It was strange, though, to think that I had someone alive and growing inside me, almost creepy. Already I felt very responsible for this new person. I ate the right foods, exercised and planned all that I would need for the baby. I worried that it may not be normal and what I would do if anything went wrong. By the time I was a couple of months pregnant I was feeling very tired and extremely weepy — if anyone said the wrong thing I either snapped at them or cried. I worried about the birth and if it would hurt.'

Many of the feelings that this woman experienced were quite normal and caused by changes in the hormones — chemical messages sent to the brain — brought about by pregnancy.

> **Reread this account and write down all the feelings that this mother had during early pregnancy. Can you think of any more feelings she might have had?**

Of course not all expectant women feel as excited as this woman did. It may be that the woman is very young or the pregnancy unwanted. Some women become pregnant again shortly after the baby is born, before they have fully recovered. Remember that planning families can be an important part of making happy families.

Above all, an expectant woman must not forget the feelings her husband might have about the pregnancy, and about being a father. It will be just as great a change for him. He may be worried about his responsibilities. Continual talk about the expected baby can be tedious, although it is important that the couple share the experience and prepare for the baby together.

In the rest of this chapter we will consider pregnancy from the point of view of the growing embryo, and follow its various stages of development in the womb. We shall also consider the parallel concerns of the mother throughout the nine months of her pregnancy.

## PREGNANCY AND THE CHILD

# Embryonic development from week 2 to week 11

During the next ten weeks the embryo changes from a microscopic speck to a recognisable shape. At ten weeks the embryo is approximately 5 cm long and about $\frac{3}{4}$ oz (18 g) in weight. This is about the weight of a letter.

All embryos follow an identical pattern of development. One step leads to the next, keeping to a special 'work plan'. Development always takes place from the head downwards. The line drawn next to the measurement indicates the length of the embryo at each stage.

---

*Week 2* .

The cluster of cells starts to curve and expand. The basis for the beginning of a recognisable shape is formed.

---

*Week 3*

2 mm  –

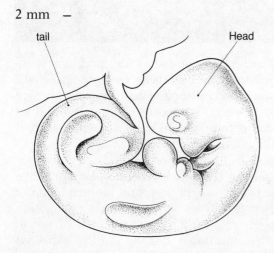

tail          Head

1 It is easy to recognise the head and tail of the embryo which is floating in a liquid called amniotic fluid. This fluid acts as a shock absorber.

2 There is a bulge below the chin which is the heart, and it has already started beating.

3 The thick spongy lining of the uterus begins to form its own blood vessels. This is called the *placenta*. The functions of the placenta are described in detail opposite. (The mother's period is now one week overdue.)

---

*Week 4*

6 mm  ——

1 The nervous system starts developing. A groove develops on the outer curve of the embryo. This groove closes to form a tube, which becomes the spinal cord. The top end swells to form the brain.

2 A large primitive opening can be seen just above the heart. This will be the mouth.

3 Early signs of ears and eyes are just visible as small bubbles. At this stage, the head and neck are half of the total length of the embryo. Rapid development now begins, at a rate of about a millimetre each day.

# PREGNANCY AND THE MOTHER

## The placenta

As the embryo develops in the uterus it needs to be kept supplied with nourishment. The placenta is formed from the thick, spongy lining of the uterus. It has its own blood vessels. The baby is joined to the placenta by a cord called the *umbilical cord*. During the nine months of pregnancy, the placenta has five important jobs to do.

*1 To provide food for the baby*  Food eaten by the mother is digested by her. The nutrients, which are the chemical substances that make up food, pass to the placenta. From the placenta the nutrients pass into the baby's bloodstream.

*2 To provide oxygen and remove carbon dioxide*  The baby does not breathe in air until after birth. In the uterus the baby receives oxygen from the mother's blood. Oxygen crosses the placenta and enters the baby's blood. Carbon dioxide passes back in the same way to the mother's blood.

*3 To remove waste products*  The baby's kidneys do not start to work until late in pregnancy. All products, e.g. excess nutrients that cannot be used by the baby, pass back across the placenta and into the mother's bloodstream.

*4 To protect the baby from illness and drugs*  The placenta can prevent many of the germs that the mother may have from harming the baby. If she has to take drugs it may prevent some of them from reaching the baby. There are some exceptions (see section on drugs in pregnancy).

*5 To produce hormones*  The placenta produces hormones which help prepare a woman's body for childbirth.

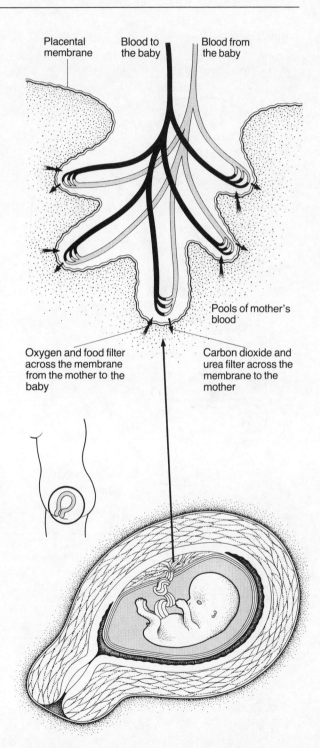

Cross-section of the placenta.

# PREGNANCY AND THE CHILD

*Week 5*

10-12mm ———

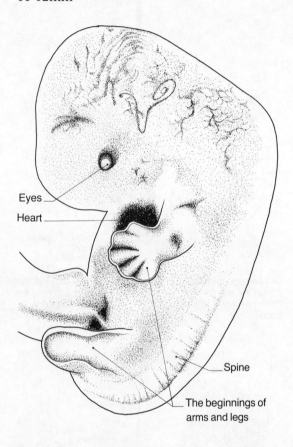

Eyes

Heart

Spine

The beginnings of
arms and legs

1  The eyes are shown as black rings.

2  The nose and cheeks begin to form under the eyes.

3  The head begins to straighten up from its very bent position.

4  Short round stalks become the beginnings of arms and legs.

5  The stem attaching the embryo to the placenta is becoming the *umbilical cord*. Through this cord, the baby receives nourishment from its mother. It also gets rid of waste products through the cord.

*Week 6*

15 mm ———

1  The liver starts producing blood cells.

2  The rather large tail between the legs begins to shrink.

3  Five finger shapes are faintly visible, though not the toes. The arms are still too short to meet.

4  There are the very beginnings of a skeleton.

5  The skin is very thin and transparent.

## PREGNANCY AND THE MOTHER

# Factors affecting embryonic development

Different things affect different stages of embryonic development. There are many crucial times when development should not be disturbed. If the schedule is interrupted, the part of the body due for development may be missing or poorly made. When we remember that many of these vital stages take place when most women do not even know they are pregnant, it is easy to realise that a mother can quite unintentionally disturb the schedule in the following ways:

## 1 Drugs and medicines in early pregnancy

While the placenta is still developing in the early weeks of pregnancy, any drug in the mother's blood may get into the baby's system as well. Not all drugs are harmful to the baby, but some are, particularly at certain stages of development. For example:

*Thalidomide* (taken to prevent nausea) — if this is taken when the limbs are developing, it can interrupt the schedule, causing deformity and stunted growth of the arms and legs. Thalidomide is no longer available although it was during the early 1960s.
*Quinine* (a pain killer) — this can cause deafness.
*Barbiturates* (a sedative) — these can reduce the oxygen supply and cause brain damage.
*Tetracycline* (an antibiotic) — this affects the development of the teeth, causing them to be stained yellow when they are eventually cut.
*Streptomycin* (an antibiotic) — this affects the hearing and balancing organs in the ears.

There are other drugs and medicines which can be dangerous for the pregnant woman and her baby. Later, when the placenta is fully formed, some drugs can still cross through to the baby and affect its development in the later stages of pregnancy.

Some women might be taking drugs permanently for certain conditions such as diabetes, epilepsy, thyroid trouble or migraine. They would need to consult their doctors before becoming pregnant, so that treatment could be adjusted if possible.

## 2 Illness: German measles

If a woman gets German measles in the first sixteen weeks of pregnancy it may cause abnormalities in the foetus. Every foetus develops in the same order, but if something interferes with the sequence, a part of development may be missed or abnormal. If the *rubella* virus, which is responsible for causing German measles, enters the bloodstream of the foetus it may interfere with the development of the eyes, ears or heart, causing severe deformity.

Now you can see why it is so important for all girls to be vaccinated against German measles while they are at school!

## 3 Diet during pregnancy

A good pattern of eating is essential for everyone all through their life. It is even more important when a woman is pregnant because she also needs to nourish her developing foetus. In particular she has a much greater need for calcium and iron than other people:

*Calcium* — the foetus needs this to build strong bones and to form teeth, even though these are still under the gums.
*Iron* — the foetus needs this to develop a healthy blood supply and to build up a store of iron. The new baby needs enough iron to last six months as its only food will be milk, which does not contain iron. Pregnant women are usually prescribed iron tablets to provide the dosage they need.

# PREGNANCY AND THE CHILD

*Week 7*

2 cm ———————

The toes begin to form.

*Week 8*
3 cm ———————

1 The muscles have begun their first exercises, allowing the embryo to make small movements.

2 The eyelids are forming.

3 The external genitals begin to appear.

4 The ears take shape.

*Weeks 9-10*

4 cm ———————————

1 The placenta is fully working.

2 All the main organs (kidneys, gut, liver, lungs, brain) have formed.

*Week 11*
5 cm ———————————————

1 The heart is completely formed, though is still very small.

2 Tooth buds appear in the mouth of the embryo.

3 The nail beds on toes and fingers are established.

4 It is possible to tell the sex.

5 The muscles are working energetically:
   a) lips open and close
   b) the forehead wrinkles
   c) the head turns
   d) amniotic fluid is swallowed
   e) arms and legs are in constant motion, but these movements are too weak to be felt by the mother

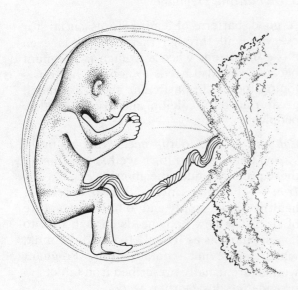

## PREGNANCY AND THE MOTHER

Many women put on too much weight during pregnancy. As well as making them feel more uncomfortable than necessary, overweight in pregnancy can result in high blood pressure, or a condition known as *toxaemia*. This was mentioned in the section on contraception (see p. 48). It is when a woman's body retains fluid and she becomes very ill. Too much weight gained in pregnancy can make the birth more difficult. It can also be difficult to lose the extra weight after the birth of the baby.

### 4 Smoking during pregnancy

It is believed that nearly 1500 babies die each year because their mothers smoked during pregnancy. Babies born to women who smoke heavily tend to be underweight and are more likely to become ill. Heavy smokers are also more likely to have a miscarriage than non-smokers.

When a mother smokes, the nicotine and carbon monoxide in the cigarette smoke go into the bloodstream. This then crosses the placenta to the foetus. Nicotine makes the blood vessels narrower so that less blood can flow through. In the placenta less blood flowing means that less food and oxygen contained in the blood will reach the foetus. Carbon monoxide joins more readily than oxygen with the red pigment (*haemoglobin*) in the blood. This means that even less oxygen reaches the foetus. The general effect of less food and oxygen on the foetus is that all development is slowed down. However, one very serious effect may be that brain cells are permanently damaged.

### 5 Alcohol during pregnancy

It is not good for a woman who is pregnant to drink too much alcohol. Alcohol is very fattening and as you have already read, too much weight gained in pregnancy is undesirable. If a pregnant woman drinks too much it may be that she is not eating enough of the right food. She may become unsteady, fall over and damage either herself or the baby. Alcohol may also affect the development of the foetus. There have even been cases of babies born with alcohol in their blood stream.

## PREGNANCY AND THE CHILD

### The foetus at 12 weeks

By twelve weeks, the developing individual is no longer an embryo, but is called a *foetus*. Everything that will be found in a fully developed human has now been established. The next stage is the period of growth and perfection of detail.

1  Approximate size 3 in. (7.5 cm). Weight 2 oz (55 g).

2  Organs are all formed, the heart beats, blood circulates and kidneys work.

3  From now on the organs grow and improve the way they function.

4  The foetus is floating in the uterus in a bag called the *amniotic sac*, full of water called *amniotic fluid*. This fluid protects the baby. (See section on amniocentesis on p. 50.)

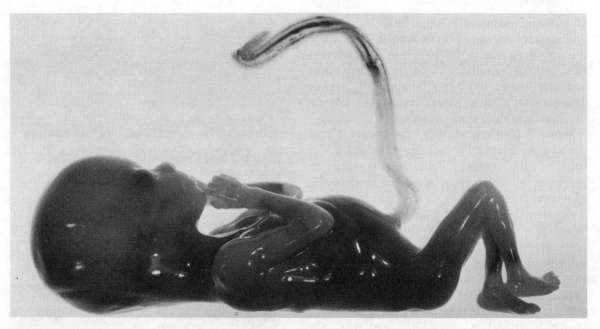

### The foetus at 16 weeks

1  Approximate size 7 in. (18 cm) long. Weight 4 oz (100 g).

2  The head is large compared to the body, almost four times the size.

3  The body appears bright red because the blood vessels glow through the transparent skin.

4  Muscles become active, although movement is negligible.

5  The foetus remains floating in amniotic fluid.

# PREGNANCY AND THE MOTHER

## Abortion

Until the foetus is 28 weeks old it can still be legally aborted in Great Britain. This is because until 28 weeks a foetus is unlikely to survive outside the womb. At this stage it cannot support its own life. Under the 1967 Abortion Act a woman may have an abortion if, in the opinion of *two* doctors, there is a risk:

1 to the life of the pregnant woman
2 of injury to her physical or mental health
3 to the physical or mental health of any other children of her family
4 of physical or mental abnormalities, or serious handicap to the unborn child

Special tests can be carried out to detect any abnormalities of the foetus, but these are carried out much earlier during pregnancy, (see p. 50). A woman may be offered an abortion on the strength of such a test's showing that her baby may be handicapped when it is born.

Abortion is a controversial subject. Some people feel that whatever the circumstances of the mother aborting a child it is the equivalent of killing it. Other people feel that certain women may not be able to look after a child, or it may be unwanted. If a child is handicapped the mother may not be able to cope with the extra commitment. They feel the woman should be able to choose what she wants. Sometimes people have religious reasons for being against abortion. What do you think about it?

## Working during pregnancy

It is very important that a pregnant woman has plenty of rest and avoids lifting heavy objects, especially towards the end of pregnancy. Consequently it is usual for a woman to stop her paid employment eleven weeks before the baby is due. At one time a woman could be dismissed for being pregnant.

Abortion march, October 1979.

# PREGNANCY AND THE CHILD

## The foetus at 20 weeks

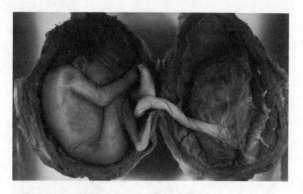

1 Approximate size 10 in. (25 cm). Weight 11 oz (300 g).

2 The skin of the foetus is getting thicker and is covered with a fine downy hair called *lanugo*. Hair may be appearing on the head, although some babies are born with very little hair.

3 Eyebrows have developed, but the eyelids remain closed.

4 First movements may now be felt by the mother.

## The foetus at 24 weeks

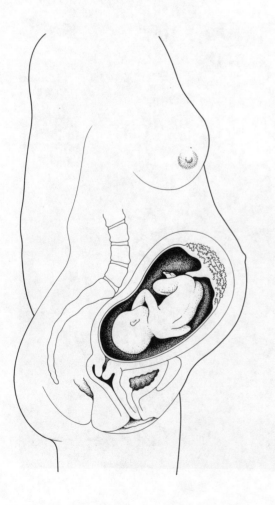

1 Approximate size 13 in. (32 cm). Weight 1 lb 7 oz (650 g).

2 The skin is less red, but wrinkled because it lacks fat.

3 The eyelids have separated, but a membrane covers the pupils, which are dull.

4 If born at this stage, the foetus will attempt to breathe, but its lungs are not properly developed and it will almost certainly die soon after birth.

---

**Design a poster for your local health centre to show some of the ways that a pregnant woman should care for her own and her unborn baby's health. You could make a different poster for all the different stages of development, picking out particular factors.**

# PREGNANCY AND THE MOTHER

In Britain, the 1980 Employment Act describes what a woman is entitled to from her employer if she gets pregnant and intends to return to work. Under this Act she is entitled to the following:

1 Continued employment until eleven weeks before the expected date of birth of the child.
2 Six weeks' pay after she stops work at the eleventh week. This pay is calculated as nine-tenths of her normal pay *less* the current amount of maternity allowance given to her by the state.
3 A return to her previous job, or another suitable similar job, up to 29 weeks after the birth of the baby. She must give her employer notice of her return by certain dates in this period.

These conditions only apply if a woman has worked continuously for two years for the same employer.

**The 1980 Employment Act lays down the minimum entitlement a woman has from her employer. Some employers give more pay to a pregnant woman if she intends to return to work. If she doesn't then return, she may have to pay her employer back.**

**Find out what your teacher's conditions of employment are relating to maternity.**

## Antenatal classes

When a woman is expecting her first baby in Britain, she is advised to attend antenatal classes. These classes help her to prepare for the birth, and teach her how to care for the baby. Sometimes mothers who already have children attend the classes. Usually, however, this is difficult unless there is someone else to look after the children. Antenatal classes begin when the woman stops work — normally eleven weeks before *confinement* (the birth). They are held weekly, often in two sessions. The first session includes preparing the mother for the birth of the baby and the second session is concerned with caring for the baby. Classes may be held at the local health centre or at the hospital.

Relaxation classes teach mothers how best to cope during the final weeks of pregnancy and during birth. The end of pregnancy is tiring because of the extra weight of the baby. Mothers are given instruction as to the best and most comfortable way to stand, sit and sleep. Correct breathing also helps a woman to relax her body. This is important during the various stages of *labour* (see p. 66).

Fathers are encouraged to attend some antenatal classes. They can learn how to change nappies, how to prepare a feed and how to bath the baby, amongst other things. They can also learn how best to help the mother during labour and childbirth.

## PREGNANCY AND THE CHILD

### The foetus at 28 weeks

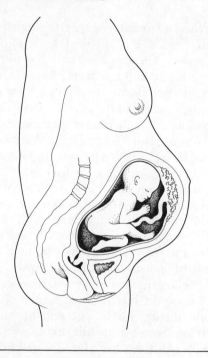

1  Approximate size 15 in. (38 cm). Weight 2 lb 2 oz (1000 g).

2  Fat has developed under the skin, which is now covered by the *vernix*. This is a white, greasy, waterproof layer which protects the skin.

3  The heart can be distinctly heard by a doctor.

4  The foetus can open its eyes. The membrane over the pupils has gone.

5  If born now the foetus could breathe, but survival would be unlikely.

### The foetus at 32 weeks

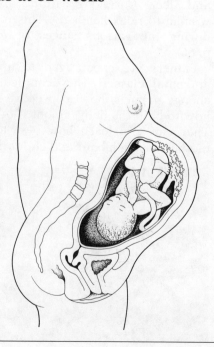

1  Approximate size 17 in. (43 cm). Weight 4 lb (1800 g).

2  The bones of the foetus head are soft and flexible, to allow the head to pass along the birth canal with less difficulty.

3  The baby is now lying in the birth position, that is in the right position for it to emerge from the woman's body. The majority of babies in the birth position lie with the head towards the lower end of the womb but see p. 72 the breech position.

4  If born now the baby could survive, given expert care in a premature baby unit (see p. 71).

## PREGNANCY AND THE MOTHER

*Parent-craft* or mother-craft classes, as they are sometimes called, provide new mothers with practical help in caring for a baby. They may include a discussion about breast-feeding versus bottle-feeding (see p. 85). They may show how to make up a bottle, following the instructions on the packet of milk.

Usually the woman is given the opportunity to bath a baby-sized doll and shown what clothes and other things a baby will need. The mother will also be shown how to fold nappies and how to make up the nappy sterilising solution.

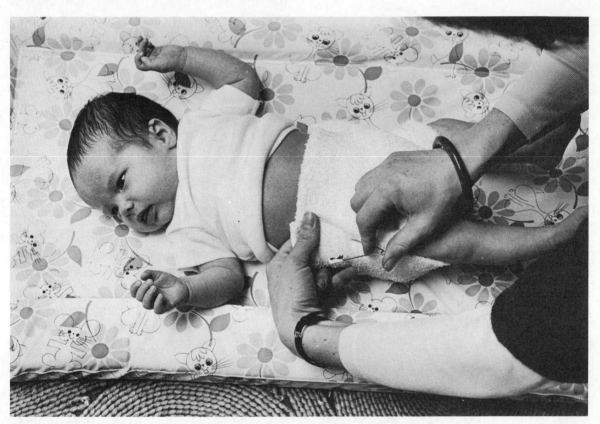

First-time mothers may also receive advice about the financial benefits available to them. In Britain these include the following:

*Maternity Allowance*

This is only paid to women who have been working. They must have paid at least six months' National Insurance contributions up to the time of stopping work. The allowance is paid for 18 weeks, beginning 11 weeks before the baby is expected, provided the

mother stops work at this time.

*Maternity grant*

This is a lump sum paid to all mothers, provided they or their husbands have paid six months' National Insurance contributions.

*Free dental treatment*

This is given to all pregnant women and mothers with babies up to one year old.

## PREGNANCY AND THE CHILD

### The foetus at 36 weeks

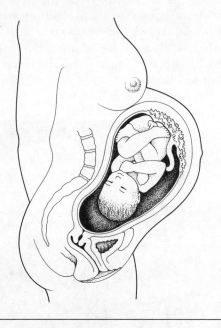

1 Approximate size $18\frac{1}{2}$ in. (46 cm) Weight $5\frac{1}{2}$ lbs (2500 g).

2 The foetus has gained more weight in the preceding four weeks. This is because fat has been deposited beneath the skin.

3 The ribs protrude less than before, while the stomach, arms and legs are much rounder.

4 To aid early feeding and sucking the cheeks have become chubby.

### The foetus at 40 weeks

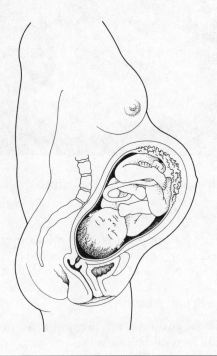

1 The pregnancy is now known as full-term and the woman can expect the birth to occur at any time around 40 weeks.

2 The baby is 20 in. long (50 cm) and weighs about 7 lb 4 oz (3300 g), although there can be wide differences in the birth weight.

3 Its skin is smooth and the lanugo has gone, except on the shoulders. However, the greasy vernix still covers the skin.

4 Its head is covered in a variable amount of hair. The skull is much firmer, but two small soft areas, one above the forehead and one at the back of the head have yet to fuse. These soft spots, known as *fontanelles* will close in the baby's first year of life.

5 The lungs are fully developed but full of amniotic fluid. When born, the lungs will fill with air.

6 A greenish-black thick substance called *muconium* fills the intestines, but will be excreted shortly after birth.

# PREGNANCY AND THE MOTHER

*Free prescriptions*

All pregnant women are entitled to free prescriptions.

## Confinement

At this stage of pregnancy, arrangements for the confinement — which is the name given to the birth — will probably have been decided. In this country most babies are born in hospital and the trend is towards hospital confinements for all mothers. Some women are particularly recommended to have hospital confinements. For example:

those having a first or fourth baby, as there is more danger associated with these births

those having twins, as the birth can be more complicated

those under 17 or over 35

those who have had any serious illness or complications during pregnancy which may affect the baby

those who need to have a Caesarean section (see p. 72)

## When things go wrong: miscarriages

About one in six fertilised eggs does not develop properly, causing the accidental failure of the pregnancy. This can happen at any time during the first 28 weeks of development, when the embryo or foetus is so undeveloped, it does not have a chance of surviving. This is called a miscarriage.

Miscarriages occur for a number of reasons. They are most likely to happen during the first three months of pregnancy. This is during the development of the embryo. Some of the causes are:

1 The cluster of cells does not successfully implant itself in the lining of the uterus.
2 Early miscarriages (before 12 weeks) usually happen because there is something seriously wrong with the developing embryo or foetus.
3 The placenta might have stopped working, causing the baby to die and miscarry.
4 The muscles around the neck of the uterus (cervix) are weak and open too early.

Miscarriages occur more often in women:

1 over 35;
2 who have failed to conceive, having tried for about six months;
3 who have already had two miscarriages.

'Although it is two years since our first baby miscarried and we now have a healthy daughter, we will always have a sense of regret for that person who we never knew or held.

At the time, we were stunned that the 14 weeks of pregnancy which had been full of hopes and plans, had so abruptly come to an end. My world seemed empty and useless. I felt weak and despondent. I was angry when I saw other couples with their babies and wondered why it had happened to us. I kept thinking back to see if I could remember what I could have done to cause the miscarriage. I had to fight back the tears when I looked after my sister's baby for the morning. I wondered if I would ever be able to have children.

When I became pregnant again, we were overjoyed, but I was worried that the same thing would happen. I was very relieved after the first 14 weeks had passed and gradually grew more confident.'

Suddenly to experience a miscarriage came as an enormous shock. What were this mother's immediate feelings? How can she help herself to think positively again?

# 5 Birth of a baby

At the end of forty weeks, in a normal pregnancy, the foetus is fully developed. It is ready to push its way into the outside world. The birth comes about through a process known as *labour*, which, as the name suggests, is to do with work. The woman works with her body to push the baby out. Labour is usually divided into three stages:

> *stage one* — contractions
> *stage two* — birth of the baby
> *stage three* — delivery of the placenta

## 1 The first stage of labour

The first stage of labour is when a woman's body prepares for the passage of the baby down the vagina and out of the body. It is usually longer for a first birth, as the muscles of the uterus are very strong before the birth. Even if the birth is going to take place in hospital, some of the time during the first stage of labour can be spent at home.

Labour may start in any one of the following ways or combination of them.

1 A *show*, that is a small discharge of blood and mucus from the vagina. The discharge will have come from the *cervix* — the opening at the base of the uterus. It formed a plug during pregnancy to help prevent the entry of germs.

2 *Contractions*, which occur when the muscles stretching from the top to the bottom of the uterus tighten. The cervix is gradually opened or *dilated* so that the baby can pass down the vagina. Early contractions may be thirty minutes apart and last less than half a minute. Towards the end of the first stage, when the cervix is fully dilated, they may be as close as every two minutes and last one and a half minutes. It is during this stage of labour that most women require some type of pain relief to help with the discomfort of the contractions (see the end of this section).

3 In the uterus, the baby is floating in and protected by amniotic fluid. This must be released before birth can occur. This is called the *breaking of the waters*.

The 'waters' may break at the beginning of labour or as the contractions grow stronger. If, however, by the end of the first stage they have not broken, then the doctor will burst the membrane to release the fluid.

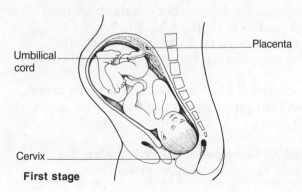

Umbilical cord
Placenta
Cervix
**First stage**

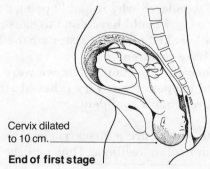

Cervix dilated to 10 cm.
**End of first stage**

## Ways of relieving the pain

If a woman has her partner with her, he can now be of great help. He can reassure her once she knows that the birth is under way. When it is time to go to hospital he can either telephone for an ambulance or take her by car. He can help by keeping her calm and making sure she has a suitcase with her, containing all the things she might want or need. In hospital he may help with pain relief, by offering her the *gas and air* as each contraction begins. Gas and air is breathed in from a mask which the woman holds. As she loses consciousness, her hand with the mask falls away and she regains consciousness. She is usually wired up to an electrical monitor which records in numbers the strength of each contraction. As the numbers appear, so her husband can tell her to use the gas and air mask.

When labour is really under way, and the contractions are strong, a woman may be offered a painkiller. *Pethidine* is one such painkiller that is often used. It is injected into a muscle, usually in the thigh. It dulls pain in about twenty minutes. The effect may last from two to five hours.

Alternatively a woman can have an almost completely painless childbirth under *epidural anaesthesia*. This is an anaesthetic injected through the muscles of a woman's back to the dura cavity in the spine. It has the effect of numbing the woman from the waist downwards. She remains conscious and can help with the birth, without the pain of contractions.

All women who attend antenatal classes are taught how to relax and breathe during labour and childbirth. A woman is shown how to control the pain she feels. These exercises can lead to what is called 'natural childbirth'. No gas or drugs to relieve the pain are used in natural childbirth.

When the cervix has dilated to ten centimetres (look at this on your ruler to see how much dilatation is necessary) the second stage of labour can begin.

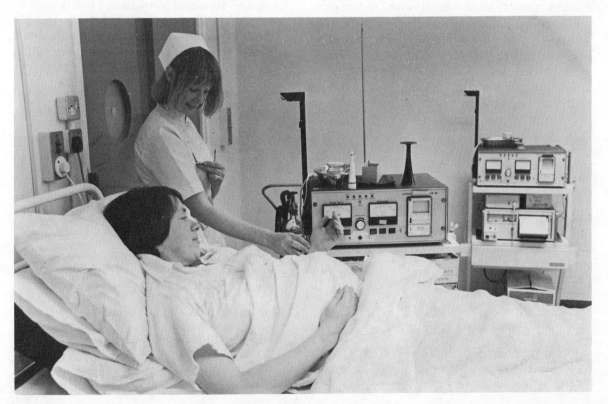

## 2 The second stage of labour

The second stage of labour is the time when the mother has to work with her body to push the baby out through the birth canal. This stage usually lasts about an hour. As each contraction now comes the mother gets a strong urge to push. As she does so, the baby moves down the birth canal (vagina). The pushing is extremely hard work and between each contraction she needs to rest. If the woman's partner is present he can help by offering her sips of water, wiping her forehead and encouraging her to push when she feels tired.

If this stage seems to be taking longer, the doctor or midwife may help pull the baby out with forceps. Forceps are like large tongs. They are placed on the baby's head and help lift the head out from the birth canal. This is called a *forceps delivery*.

Delivering the head of the baby is the most difficult part of the birth. If necessary, a small cut can be made in the entrance to the vagina, under local anaesthetic, to enlarge the opening. This is called an *episiotomy*. The cut is stitched up again after the birth. Once the head has been born the baby's mouth and nose will be cleaned of mucus and she (or he) may being to breathe. A final push usually delivers the baby.

These are the feelings experienced by one man at the birth of his first child.

'To be present at the birth of my child was a very emotional and unforgettable experience. From the moment the waters burst at home in bed, through the late night phone call to the hospital and drive to the maternity unit my memories remain very vivid. I really had to make an effort to keep calm, whilst all the while I felt very, very excited. The silent unending waiting during which the formalities were undertaken. Then the long interval between those initial contractions and the unbelievable glimpse of my daughter's head.

As my wife turned from side to side, so I moved round the bed to be ready with the gas and air. All the time my attention was upon the monitor displaying the baby's heart-beat and the strength of contractions. At 6.55 a.m. came that first view of the baby's head. At 7.30 a.m. a doctor and two junior midwives arrived. The small room seemed suddenly crowded. Finally at 7.45 a.m. my daughter was safely born. My emotions reached a peak as my wife and I cuddled that newborn infant, and called her by name, Hello, little Sarah.'

## What it feels like to be born

For nine months the unborn baby lies in a warm, dark uterus or *womb*, curled up listening to the sounds of its mother's body. The way into the outside world is down a tight, but elastic passageway. There is just enough room and none to spare. Imagine yourselves being squeezed for several hours along a warm, dark, wet tube.

Most babies are born in hospital, in what is called a *delivery room*. This is a room where all the equipment is close by to ensure a safe delivery. Delivery rooms have traditionally been brightly lit and sometimes quite noisy. There are instructions, talk, machines, cries of pain or relief. The baby's head is born. Immediately her (or his) mouth and nose are cleaned out. She may be lifted up, dangled in the air and the cord cut quickly, which is not painful. This cord is called the *umbilical cord* and attaches the baby's stomach to the placenta in the uterus. The baby's mouth and nose are cleaned again of any mucus and drops are put in her eyes to clean them. Then the baby is weighed and wrapped in towels.

A French doctor, called Frederick Leboyer believes that what a baby feels at birth is important. He describes how a newborn baby should be treated. Leboyer thinks that the lights should be as low as possible. Everyone should be quiet, talking in whispers. When the baby is delivered, and before the cord is cut, the child should be placed on the mother's stomach. Leboyer believes that the baby feels warmth from its mother's stomach and is reassured by her heart-beat. He also suggests that every mother should massage her baby and so get to know how the child feels. The baby will also get to know her mother.

Some people prefer one method of delivery, others another. It is up to the mother to choose the one with which she feels more happy. In many hospitals nowadays the delivery room is somewhere between these two.

**Copy and complete the chart below to compare life in the womb with birth in a hospital delivery room and birth in a Leboyer delivery room.**

| | Life in the womb | Birth in a traditional hospital delivery room | Birth in a Leboyer delivery room |
|---|---|---|---|
| What position is the baby in? | | | |
| What can the baby feel? | | | |
| What light does the baby see? | | | |
| What sounds can the baby hear? | | | |

When the umbilical cord has been cut, the baby is carefully washed and thoroughly examined to ensure that everything is fully developed.

## 3 The third stage of labour

The very strong contractions of the second stage of labour stop when the baby is born. A few minutes later the contractions start again so that the placenta can be delivered. Allowing the baby to suck at the breast can sometimes help with this stage as it makes the uterus contract. The uterus becomes smaller as it contracts and the placenta separates from it. A final contraction, with the mother pushing is usually enough to complete the process of birth.

The placenta and membranes attached to it are examined thoroughly. The midwife checks that no parts have broken away and been left in the womb. Here they may cause pain and bleeding. It is vital that the placenta is delivered as it is no longer of use in the mother's body.

## After the birth

In hospital, after being washed, the baby usually sleeps in a plastic crib beside the mother's bed. The mother can pick her baby out from the crib to change, feed and hold her. She can also see her baby through the sides of the transparent crib. The mother and baby may stay in hospital from two to five days. It is in these first days that mother and baby need to get to know each other. It is important for the mother to hold her baby. Forming this early relationship is known as *bonding*.

### The baby

The baby is carefully examined in the mater-nity hospital. Doctors who specialise in caring for babies are called *paediatricians*. They carry out special tests to ensure the baby is fully healthy before it is discharged from hospital. They test some of the baby's reflexes, such as:

*Rooting* — when the sides of the baby's mouth are gently stroked she turns her head towards the touch and purses her mouth.
*Sucking* — when a nipple-like object is put in her mouth she sucks.
*Falling* (Moro) — if the baby feels she is falling she throws out her arms and legs. She opens her hands and may cry.
*Hand grasp* — if an object or finger touches the palm of the baby's hand, she closes her hand around the object or finger. The grasp may be strong enough for the baby to be lifted up.

### The mother

During her time in the maternity hospital the mother will be given further instructions about caring for herself and her new baby. These will include exercises to help her

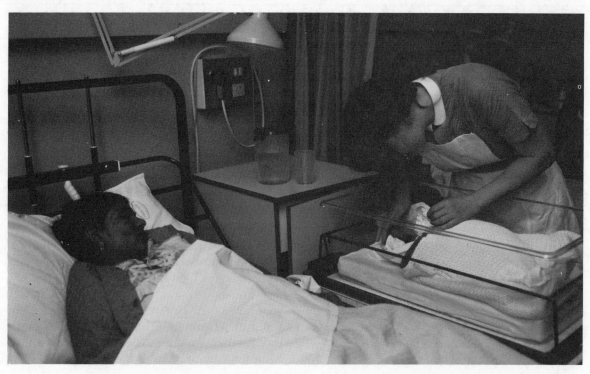

regain her shape after the birth. If a mother breastfeeds her baby she often regains her figure quickly. Midwives will help the woman to breastfeed or bottle-feed her baby. They will also show her how to bath the baby, and give other helpful advice.

It is usual for a family planning specialist to visit the mother before she leaves hospital. The specialist will advise her as to which methods of family planning are available if she wants them, and when to resume intercourse. If a woman is breastfeeding her baby there is a special contraceptive pill available. This does not interfere with her milk supply. Despite family planning advice it is not unknown for a woman to be pregnant when she attends her postnatal examination six weeks after the birth.

## Complications at birth

### Premature and small babies

Babies who weigh less than $5\frac{1}{2}$ lb (2.5 kg), are considered to be underweight. Such babies are in need of special care, known as *intensive care*. Babies who are born too early are often underweight and are known as *premature babies*. These are babies born before the 36th week of pregnancy. The bones of a premature baby's skull are still very soft, so the baby must be delivered with great care to avoid damage to the brain.

Immediately after the birth, a premature baby is usually put into an *incubator*. An incubator is a small enclosed unit which is completely sterile and free from infection (see photo). Inside the incubator the baby is kept at a constant temperature and humidity and fed with a constant supply of oxygen. It is still possible for a mother to help care for her baby while the child is in special care. The mother may touch and feel her baby by putting her hand into gloves in the side of the incubator. She may not touch the baby directly though, since this might mean the risk of infection. She can visit her child frequently. She can keep her breastmilk supply

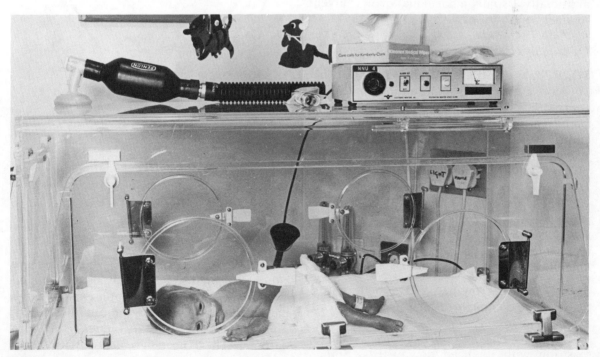

A baby in an incubator.

going by using a breast pump. She may be allowed to help change the baby's nappy inside the incubator. The baby usually stays in the incubator until she is strong enough to survive outside.

Some babies are referred to as *small-for-dates*. This means that they are fully formed, but are small when they are born. Small-for-dates babies have normally been under-fed in the uterus. The placenta has failed to supply the baby with enough food and oxygen. Multiple-birth babies are usually small-for-dates. Babies born to mothers who smoke are sometimes small because they have been deprived of oxygen (see p. 57). Small-for-dates babies are often put in incubators for a short time.

## Induction

If it is necessary to start labour artificially then the mother is *induced*. Induction is usually only necessary when a baby is more than two weeks overdue, if the placenta stops working, or if the mother has high blood pressure, toxaemia or diabetes. Labour can be induced by the doctor breaking the waters artificially. Usually a hormonal drug is given to start contractions.

## Caesarean section

When baby is born by this method the surgeon cuts through the abdomen to the uterus. The baby is lifted from the mother's body. The placenta is removed at the same time. The cut edges of the mother's skin are drawn together and either stitched or clipped. In the past a general anaesthetic has been usual for this operation. Nowadays it can be carried out under epidural anaesthetic with the mother conscious. The cut can be made low to leave a 'bikini line' scar.

A woman may need to have a Caesarean birth because:

1 She has a narrow pelvis. The bone joints will not give enough to let the baby's head pass through.
2 The baby has not settled into the birth position with its head downwards. Some-

times it lies in the uterus with its bottom downwards. This is called the *breech position*. Doctors can sometimes move the baby round. If the doctor cannot turn the baby round, it may be born bottom first. This is known as a breech birth. Sometimes the cervix will not open wide enough for the baby to come out and a Caesarean section needs to be performed.

Breech position.

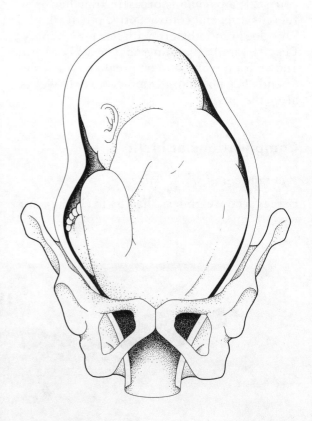

3 The mother may also have high blood pressure or toxaemia (see p. 57).

## Still births

Sometimes babies are born dead. These are called still births. Death may have occurred late on in pregnancy by, for example, the baby being strangled by the umbilical cord. This is always a great sadness for both parents. They need great sympathy and understanding from all those around them at this difficult time.

## A healthy baby?

Usually the first two questions that parents ask when their baby is born are 'Is it a boy or girl?' and 'Is it healthy?'

The risks of a baby not being normal at birth are very small. Any abnormality present at birth is called a *congenital disorder* or birth defect. There are many different sorts of congenital disorder; some are minor, others are more serious.

Congenital disorders can arise in three different ways.

1 Some run in families and are inherited through genes. If in either parent there is an abnormal gene, then there is always a *chance* that the baby will also have one, e.g. haemophilia.
2 Some occur because of failure in development before birth, e.g. hare lip. This usually happens during the embryonic stage (the first 12 weeks) during which time all the basic organs and tissues develop.
3 Some are caused by an injury to the baby during birth, e.g. cerebral palsy.

The first cause above is called a *genetic* cause. These disorders are inherent in the baby and are a defect in the genes and or chromosomes that the child possesses. The second and third causes above are usually what are called *environmental* causes. Environmental causes are those where the surroundings of the child influence the developmental process. Remember the surroundings are not just the physical whereabouts but things like viruses as well (see p. 55). Sometimes environmental factors and genetic factors work together. That is, the environment can cause a change in the genes of the baby. The result is then a genetic disorder that is caused by the environment. It is often very difficult to give a clear and definite reason for a birth defect. It is rather like a car crash. The cause is sometimes uncertain. Were the brakes defective? Had the driver been drinking? Did the wet road make the car skid? Or was it a combination of these? Sometimes, abnormalities are caused in more than one way. Here again we have to consider genetic and environmental causes (nature and nurture). It is sometimes difficult to distinguish between the two. Over the past fifty years we have found out a lot more

A Mongol child painting at the John F. Kennedy Centre.

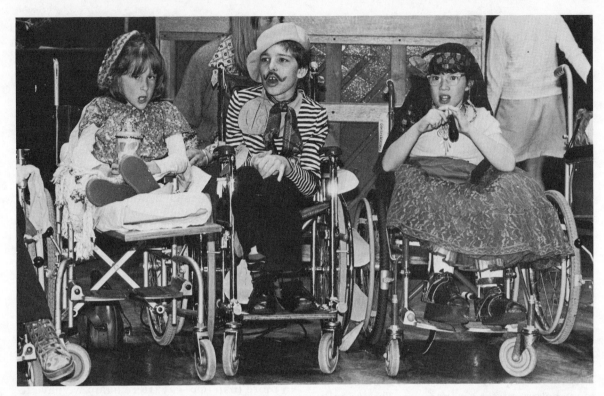

about congenital handicaps and their causes but there is still much work to be carried out. The chart shows the main names of con-genital disorders on the left-hand side and gives the causes which we know contribute to the abnormalities.

| Congenital disorder | Cause | | | | | |
|---|---|---|---|---|---|---|
| | Abnormal genes | Parents' blood groups | Virus infection | Drugs | Damage to brain at birth | Alcohol | Developmental failure/causes unknown |
| Haemophilia | * | | | | | |
| Mongolism (Downs' syndrome) | * | | | | | |
| Cystic fibrosis | * | | | | | |
| Rhesus problem babies | | * | | | | |
| Spina bifida | * | | | * | | |
| Hydrocephalus | | | | * | | |
| Congenital heart disease | | | * | | | * |
| Hare lip and cleft palate | | | | | | | * |
| Cerebral palsy (spastic) | | | | | * | |
| Some mental handicap | | | * | * | * | |
| Blindness | | | * | | | |
| Deafness | | | * | | | |

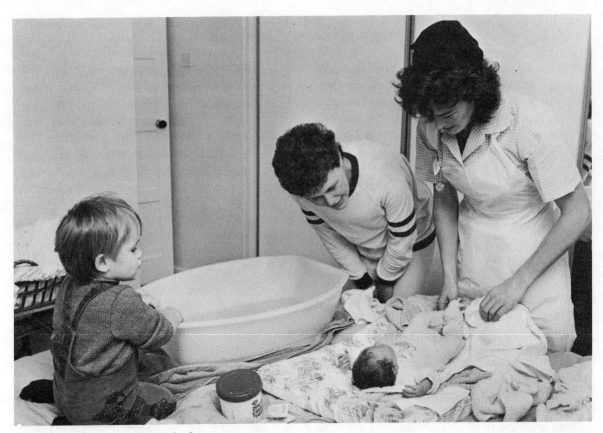

A visit from the community midwife.

## The new baby at home

When a new mother first arrives home she is advised to rest and perhaps stay in bed for a few days. There are ways in which the new family is supported by organisations in Britain. The community midwife visits the mother daily from the first day at home, until ten days after the birth. Each day the midwife cleans and re-dresses the baby's umbilical cord which is healing. She will check that the mother is well and help her to feed and bath the baby. Through this time her partner and any other members of her family can help with the new tasks involved. Friends and neighbours can help by visiting and sending cards. In many families it is the grandmother who comes to stay to keep the new mother company and help with the work.

About ten days after the birth the health visitor will take over from the midwife. The health visitor will explain the system of child health clinics. She will tell the mother when they are open, what happens there and what is available to buy. She will explain what injections and *immunisations* (protection from disease) are available in the baby's first year.

A new mother will often visit the clinic weekly to check the baby's weight. She will also get general advice about caring for the baby. Appointments are made for the mother and baby to visit the paediatrician to check the baby's developmental progress.

In addition mothers receive financial aid in the form of Child Benefit. This is a weekly allowance for each child in the family under sixteen, or under eighteen if still in full-time education. Some mothers pick this up from their local Post Office once a week. Others receive a cheque in the post at the end of each month. It is intended to help with the cost of child-rearing. As you know, bringing up children is expensive.

There are also various voluntary postnatal support groups which help the new mother. One such group in Britain is the National Childbirth Trust. They run a breastfeeding counselling service — mothers who are having problems with breastfeeding can ring their local counsellor for advice and support. They also publish information leaflets on practical matters that affect the new mother and her baby.

### The postnatal check

Six weeks after the birth of the baby, either the woman's doctor or the hospital give her a thorough examination. This is to check that her body is returning to normal. The doctor will give her an internal examination of her vagina and uterus, and generally checks the woman's state of health. He also checks on her progress with feeding and caring for the baby. If she is having any problems, for example if she feels depressed or tired, the woman can discuss these with the doctor.

Now is the time when a woman and her husband need to decide what type of contraceptive device they will use if they do not want another child immediately. It is wrong to believe that breastfeeding will stop a woman becoming pregnant again. It does not.

## Love at first sight?

Many mothers are shocked by the sight of their newborn baby. The baby is not usually very attractive. In the photograph this baby is four weeks old and looks quite different from when she was born.

The birth process, especially a first birth, can be long, painful and very tiring for the mother. Love may be the last thing that she feels. While still physically exhausted she is plunged straight into a twenty-four hour job

with no time off in the weeks to follow. This may hardly give her time to consider her own feelings towards her baby.

Most women feel protective towards their babies in the early weeks. Learning to love a baby as a person comes gradually. The baby settles down. The mother's life returns to normal and the baby begins to respond more and more to her and her partner.

---

**A group of mothers met at a postnatal clinic. This is how they described their early experiences with their babies.**

'I felt very proud of Dominic and wanted to show him to everyone. At that stage he was more of a possession than someone I loved.'

'I had a very difficult birth and felt exhausted. Sarjit woke every three hours for milk, for six weeks, night and day. Never did I have more than a couple of hours unbroken sleep. I was too tired to enjoy him.'

'For the first few days I felt full of happiness. Then, on the tenth morning the baby seemed to cry for hours, demanding food, wanting to be picked up, changed and cuddled. Nothing in the house got done. There was no time to myself, not even for lunch. When my husband came home he joked that I was still in my dressing gown. I burst into tears. At that point I regretted ever having had Rachel'.

'Mark cried for hours on end. Sometimes it was all through the night. I felt so inadequate because I didn't know what to do. At times I could have happily tossed him out the window. I was that frustrated.'

Make a list of the different feelings that each mother had towards her baby. If you have older sisters or cousins ask them how they felt in those early weeks at home with a new baby. Add their feelings to your list. Why do you think some mothers feel frustrated with their new babies?

## Father's share

It is important that the new father gets to know his baby as soon as possible. He needs to build his own relationship with his new daughter or son. The new mother and baby need his help and care at this time. The father must help organise the running of the home.

New fathers need to learn, just as new mothers do, how to care for a young child, and the two parents must work together. Both must adjust to the new member of the family. Sometimes the father will stay at home while the mother goes back to her job. Sometimes the mother may not have a partner to help her. In these families friends become more important than ever for the company and support they bring at this time.

Mothers must let their partners share in the caring of the baby. In some cases the father might feel left out if all the mother's attention is on the baby. Which of the following jobs do you think that both partners can share?

| | |
|---|---|
| feeding the baby | shopping for the baby's needs |
| bathing the baby | shopping for food and household goods |
| changing the baby | cooking meals |
| taking the baby for a walk | tidying the house |
| playing with the baby | doing the family laundry |
| washing nappies | paying the bills |
| putting the baby to bed | cleaning the home |

Of course, all these jobs can be done by both men and women. If the mother is tired or worried though, then the father must be able to offer her support and comfort. This is a most important way in which the new three-way relationship is set up.

## Another baby in the family

It is very difficult for a small child who is still very dependent on her parents for most needs, to learn to share her mother and father with someone else. The arrival of a new baby is bound to make changes in a child's life. The

child may feel jealous as a result of these changes. Try to think how a young child might feel when her mother goes away for a few days and comes home with a tiny baby. The baby may be crying loudly when the child wants to be quiet. The baby may need feeding when her sister wants her mother to play. Everyone may make a fuss about the baby and the child may feel left out.

The child can be made to feel part of all the new activity if she is allowed to help look after the baby. Young children develop good feelings towards their new baby sister or brother if their own feelings are also considered. A mother can help prepare her child for the arrival of a new baby. She can spend time talking about what it will be like with a baby in the house. Using photographs of when the child was a baby or borrowing books from the library can help explanations. It may be that the mother has never gone away and left her child for any time before. She will need to prepare her family for this. Staying with grandparents for a short time is a way of preparing a child. Getting the child used to spending time alone with her father is also important. Most hospitals allow children to visit in the afternoon and a special present from the baby to the child can be a good introduction.

At home older children need time on their own with the mother. She needs to set aside a time to be alone with each child. This is usually possible when the baby is asleep. Older children will need more love and reassurance than usual. They will also need time to talk about their feelings towards their new sister or brother. Above all, involving a child in caring for the baby will help to develop a bond between the two children.

---

**There is a lot a young child can do to help if it is allowed, although it might take longer than the mother or father would. Even a two-year-old can help to fetch things. Make a list of at least ten things a small child can do to help care for the baby.**

---

# 6 Physical development

Physical development is the growth of the body and changes in appearance that occur during life. The body grows most rapidly in the period before birth and in the first few years of life. During the nine months of pregnancy one tiny cell develops into a fully formed human baby. By the time a child is 6 months old she will have doubled her birth weight and at $2\frac{1}{2}$ years old she will be roughly half her adult height. So a child who is three feet tall at $2\frac{1}{2}$ will probably be six feet tall as an adult.

As the child grows older the rate of physical development slows down. Physical changes still occur throughout life. The same person will look very different at different ages. During the teenage years the sexual organs mature. At the same time other changes take place. Boys' voices break and their beards start growing. Girls' bodies change shape

with the development of breasts and rounding of the hips. In later life people's hair goes grey and skin becomes wrinkled. Muscles become weaker and bones more fragile.

These are natural changes that happen to all people. Throughout life people's physical development is affected both by the genes inherited from their parents, and by their surroundings. This means therefore that both environmental and genetic factors are involved.

## Development before birth

### Genetic influences

At the moment of conception the new embryo receives genes from both parents. Some of these genes affect physical appearance and development. Hair, eye and skin colouring are determined by genes. Some physical disorders, like haemophilia and the Rhesus factor in the blood (see p. 74), are also genetically inherited from parents.

Sometimes a mistake occurs when the sperm or egg cell are formed or when they come together at conception. This may cause the genes of the foetus to be abnormal. The condition called Downs' syndrome is the result of this type of mistake (see p. 109).

### Environmental influences

The environment is the immediate world a person lives in. Before birth the mother's body is the environment for the developing foetus. The mother's womb is a very stable, or unchanging, place. The foetus is kept at a constant temperature with a good supply of

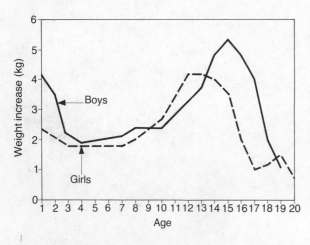

The annual increase in weight for girls and boys between the ages of 1 and 20. This increase varies during the period of growth and is greatest during puberty.

oxygen and the food for growth. It is well protected from the outside world (see p. 53).

However, the changing state of the mother's health may alter this environment and damage the foetus. If the mother is malnourished or undernourished, the foetus may not get enough food to grow properly and may be small when born. Also the child may not have received enough iron in her blood to carry oxygen to all parts of her body. This condition is called anaemia. The developing foetus may be affected by drugs taken by the mother. As you have already read in the chapter on pregnancy, one drug, called Thalidomide, had a very serious effect on physical development. Pregnant women who took this drug gave birth to babies whose arms and legs were deformed or missing. Babies born to women who smoke have a lower birth weight than babies born to non-smoking mothers. A woman who is under stress may give birth to a premature baby.

### Combined effects of genes and the environment

Usually it is not possible to tell whether a characteristic is caused by genetic or environmental factors. A person's genes and environment may both affect the same aspect of physical development, e.g. height. A man may have inherited genes to make him tall. However if he does not have a good diet his growth may be stunted. Genetic and environmental factors also interact before birth. A newborn baby girl may be small not because she inherited genes to make her small, but because she did not receive enough nourishment in the womb.

## Development after birth

### Genetic influences

Throughout life physical development is affected by a person's genes. Some genetic effects will only be seen later in life, e.g. the shape of teeth, the age of becoming sexually mature and of hair turning grey.

### Environmental influences

Before birth the baby received everything she needed from her mother. At birth she moved from the warm, safe surroundings of her mother's body to the outside world where she must do certain things for herself. In order to survive she has to start breathing on her own, sucking to obtain food, digesting food and excreting waste material. The baby also has to draw attention to herself by crying so that the people around her will see to her needs. Although she has started doing some things for herself she is still very helpless. The people who care for her have to make sure that she gets what she needs from the world. They have to provide an environment that helps her physical development.

For physical development a baby needs:

1 a good diet
2 activity, exercise and play
3 sleep and rest
4 warmth
5 health care
6 protection from danger

## 1 A good diet

### Why the body needs food

A good diet is one that contains the correct *nutrients* in the right amounts. Nutrients are chemicals in food that everyone needs to keep their bodies healthy and working properly. Different nutrients are needed by the body for different reasons:

*1 Growth* Babies and young children are growing rapidly and they need particular nutrients to build their bones and muscles as they grow.
*2 Repair* Throughout life worn-out cells of the body are replaced by new ones. Parts of the body that have been damaged are repaired. Particular nutrients are necessary for this renewal and repair.

*3 Energy* Even a very young baby is active, kicking, crying and moving about. She becomes more active as she starts to crawl and walk. People need particular nutrients to provide energy for physical activity. The same nutrients supply energy for essential body functions like breathing and the beating of the heart. These nutrients are also used to keep the body warm.

*4* Some nutrients provide materials for healthy bones, teeth, skin and blood and for good vision.

The following table gives the names of important nutrients and the reason why the body needs each of them. If the diet does not contain enough of a nutrient, the person's health will be affected. Different foods contain different nutrients.

*Table of nutrients*

| Nutrient | Reason body needs this nutrient |
| --- | --- |
| **Protein** | For growth of new cells and repair of damaged cells. Soft tissues like muscles, brain and liver are composed mainly of protein. |
| **Carbohydrates** Starch and sugar | As sources of energy which is 'burnt' in the body's muscles. A by-product of energy metabolism is heat. |
| **Fats** | For very high energy value |
| **Vitamins** Vitamin A | For vision |
| Vitamin B complex | Making red blood cells, releasing energy from food and allowing normal body processes to take place. |
| Vitamin C | Important in healing wounds and forming firm muscle. Helps body to absorb iron from food. |
| Vitamin D | Helps to lay down calcium in bones and teeth. |
| **Minerals** Calcium | Builds strong bones and teeth. |
| Iron | Forms haemoglobin in red blood cells. It is the haemoglobin which carries oxygen to the brain. |
| Phosphorous | For bones and teeth |
| Fluoride | Protects teeth of young children against decay. |
| **Dietary fibre** (Roughage) | Helps remove waste material from the body by stimulating large intestine. |

| Signs of deficiency | Good sources |
|---|---|
| Deficiency causes the child to be physically under-developed and prevents normal development of brain. Absence of protein causes cells to take up water and swell. Protein deficiency causes kwashiorkor. | Meat, fish, eggs, milk, cheese, peas, beans, lentils, cereals |
| Child is underweight and lethargic. | Cereals: e.g. breakfast cereal, rice, pasta, oatmeal, bread and wheat flour, potatoes, sugar |
| See above | Milk, butter, margarine, liver, spinach |
| Mild deficiency leads to poor vision at night. Severe deficiency in childhood leads to blindness. | Milk, butter, margarine, liver, spinach |
| Deficiency causes child to be lethargic. Diseases caused include pellagra, beri beri and anaemia. | Milk, cereals, peas, beans, lentils, spinach |
| Deficiency leads to cracked lips, bleeding gums. Absence of Vitamin C retards growth in children and causes scurvy. | Fresh fruit (especially citrus fruits and blackcurrants) and vegetables |
| The young child's bones do not harden. The bones bend and joints become swollen. This disease is called rickets. (In teenagers the absence of Vitamin D may be incorrectly called 'growing pains'.) | Sunshine on skin, butter, milk, eggs, cheese, margarine, oily fish, e.g. halibut and cod |
| Same as Vitamin D | Cheese, milk, eggs, wheat flour, oatmeal, green vegetables |
| Tiredness and irritability. This disorder is called anaemia. | Red meat, liver, eggs, wholewheat flour, pulses |
| Deficiency is very rare. | Cheese, milk, liver, kidney, bread, eggs |
| Teeth are less resistant to decay. (Flouride is especially important in countries where children eat large quantities of sweets.) | Water supplies to which flouride has been added, some toothpastes, China tea |
| A diet low in fibre leads to constipation and sometimes diseases of the bowel and stomach. | Green vegetables, fresh fruit, wholemeal bread and cereals. |

## Eating to excess

While foods are necessary for a healthy life, eating too much of some foods can be harmful. If too much of the energy-rich foods is eaten the extra food is stored in the body as fat. Fat babies are more likely to develop bronchial infections.

We eat many different kinds of sugar. There is the sugar we add to tea and coffee, cakes, jam and biscuits, sugar in milk, and sugar in fruit. Refined sugars have been treated and can lead to tooth decay, but natural sugars, such as those present in fruit, do not. Why is refined sugar so damaging? On the teeth there is a layer of bacteria called plaque which changes sugary foods into acid. The acid attacks the hard enamel of the tooth and makes holes. The bacteria can then reach the soft pulp of the tooth, the tooth starts to decay and the person gets toothache. The pain occurs because the nerves in the pulp are irritated by the decay. When the decay is severe an abcess may form at the root of the tooth.

The stages of tooth decay.

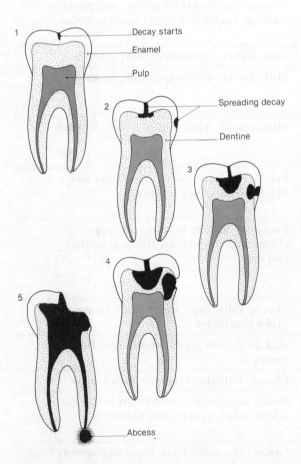

1 Decay starts
Enamel
Pulp
2 Spreading decay
Dentine
3
4
5 Abcess

**Sweets are sometimes given to children as a reward. Sometimes they are used as a bribe.**

**What else could Emma's mother have bought her instead of chocolate?**

## Feeding a baby

For the first four to six months of life milk is the baby's only food. So in order to survive and be healthy she has to get all the essential nutrients from milk. A baby may be fed on her mother's milk or on specially prepared formula milk powder. Human milk naturally contains all the nutrients a baby needs in the correct balance. Formula milk is made from cow's milk that has been modified to make it more like human milk. This milk too has the right mixture of the nutrients a baby needs. Ordinary pasteurised milk contains the right balance of nutrients for a young calf but a young human baby cannot digest it properly.

A baby in the first few months of life has to be fed every three or four hours. Some mothers feed their babies when they are hungry. This is called demand feeding. Other mothers feed their babies at set times. This is schedule feeding. If the mother tries to feed according to a schedule that matches the baby's demands she then knows when the next feed is going to be and she can plan her time better.

*Breastfeeding*

For the first few days after giving birth a mother's breasts produce *colostrum*. This

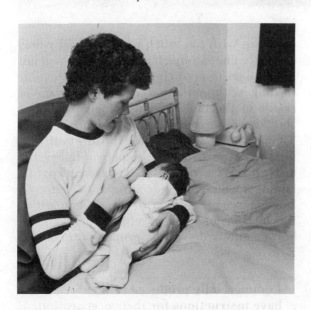

liquid gives the new baby water, a little sugar, minerals and antibodies. The antibodies are important because they help the baby's body to fight infections. Colostrum builds up in the breasts towards the end of pregnancy in preparation for the new baby. The mother does not produce milk until the

baby is about three days old. The action of the baby sucking on the nipple stimulates the glands in the mother's breast to produce milk. The more the baby sucks, the more milk the mother produces.

Mothers choose to breastfeed for several reasons.

1 They find it is more convenient. Milk is continually available so the baby can be fed at any time. There is no need to spend time sterilising bottles and making up feeds. Breastfeeding does mean that the mother is the only person who can feed the baby — no one else can do it for her.

2 They feel it is the natural thing to do. The mother's breasts produce milk with the right ingredients at the right temperature for the baby. During pregnancy the mother's body laid down fat reserves for feeding her baby. By breastfeeding she can get her figure back more quickly.

3 Breast milk is sterile, that is free from bacteria and viruses. This reduces the chances of the baby getting an intestinal infection such as gastro-enteritis.

4 Breastfeeding can be a pleasurable experience. In the first few weeks mother and baby are developing a relationship or attachment to each other. Close contact gives the baby feelings of warmth and comfort. Breastfeeding helps to form this bond.

---

"WOMAN TOLD NOT TO BREASTFEED HER BABY IN TRAIN."

**Why do you think the fellow-passengers objected to the mother breastfeeding her baby?**

**Decide whether you agree with the mother, or the person who told her to stop breastfeeding. Write a letter to the newspaper supporting the person of your choice and saying why you support them.**

---

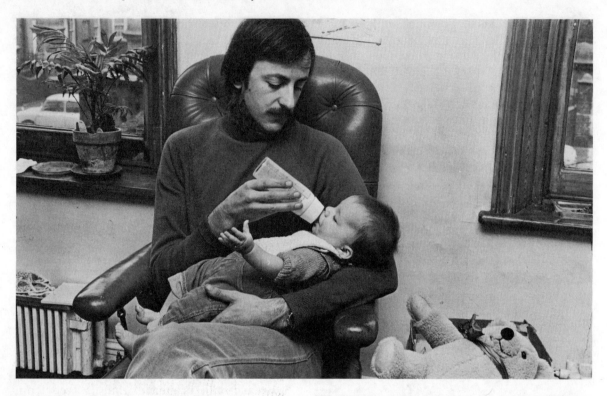

## Bottle-feeding

In the past many babies became ill and died if the mother died in childbirth or was unable to feed the baby herself. Some babies survived because they were breastfed by another woman, called a *wet-nurse*. Other babies were fed on goat's milk or cow's milk. However, people did not know enough about the need to sterilise the milk to kill bacteria, so these babies often became ill and died.

Today the situation is very different. Bottle-feeding is a perfectly safe alternative to breastfeeding provided the milk is prepared in clean conditions. Several brands of baby milk are on sale in supermarkets and chemists. On the packets are instructions for making up the milk and information about the amount of milk to be given to babies of different ages. It is important to follow these instructions carefully. If extra milk-powder is added the baby will be given too much food, which may make her fat. She will also receive too much salt which may be difficult for her body to get rid of. When the feed is made up with too much water the baby may eat so that her stomach is full, but she will not have taken in enough nourishment. Regular feeding with milk that is too dilute could result in the baby being malnourished and slow down her growth.

Proper sterilisation of the feeding bottles is vital because to keep the baby healthy the milk must be free of bacteria. Sterilising tablets or liquids for feeding bottles are on sale. These are simple to use and provided the instructions are carefully followed the bottles and teats will be properly sterilised.

---

**Commercially produced milk-powders have instructions for their preparation.**

**1 Why may it be difficult for an adult to follow these instructions?**
**2 What may be the effect on the baby if the instructions are not carefully followed?**

---

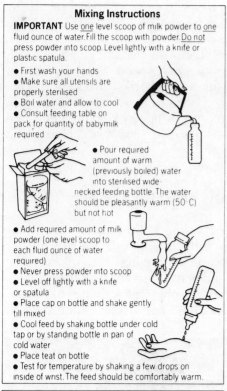

### Mixing Instructions

**IMPORTANT** Use <u>one</u> level scoop of milk powder to <u>one</u> fluid ounce of water. Fill the scoop with powder. <u>Do not</u> press powder into scoop. Level lightly with a knife or plastic spatula.

- First wash your hands
- Make sure all utensils are properly sterilised
- Boil water and allow to cool
- Consult feeding table on pack for quantity of babymilk required
- Pour required amount of warm (previously boiled) water into sterilised wide-necked feeding bottle. The water should be pleasantly warm (50°C) but not hot
- Add required amount of milk powder (one level scoop to each fluid ounce of water required)
- Never press powder into scoop
- Level off lightly with a knife or spatula
- Place cap on bottle and shake gently till mixed
- Cool feed by shaking bottle under cold tap or by standing bottle in pan of cold water
- Place teat on bottle
- Test for temperature by shaking a few drops on inside of wrist. The feed should be comfortably warm.

### Mixing and storing a whole day's feed

You can do this by making up each feed in separate bottles or by making up the total amount for the day in a special sterilised jug with a secure lid and transferring to bottles. (Always use one level scoop per fluid ounce of water.) Store milk in refrigerator with caps on bottles. Use within 24 hours. Before use, warm feed by standing bottle in hot water. Then shake bottle to ensure feed is thoroughly mixed for your baby.

Mothers choose to bottle-feed for several reasons.

1 They may be unable to breastfeed. Some mothers produce insufficient milk or have problems with their nipples.
2 It is more convenient. If a mother returns to work shortly after the baby is born, the person who cares for the baby can feed her while the mother is away. The mother is not always tied down by feeding times.
3 They feel breastfeeding in public is embarrassing, so they choose to bottle-feed, which they feel they can do anywhere.
4 Other people can help feed the baby. This gives father, grandparents and even older brothers and sisters the chance to join in this aspect of caring for the baby.

**Sheila and Richard are expecting their first baby. They are talking about whether the baby will be breast or bottle-fed. Richard thinks the baby should be breastfed. Sheila would like to bottle-feed.**

**What do you think each is saying?**

### Water

Normally the baby's milk contains all the water she needs. However when the weather is hot she may become thirsty and cry. She will become even more thirsty if she is given milk. Some boiled water that has been cooled down will quench her thirst.

### Weaning

Teaching a baby to eat foods other than liquids is called weaning. In the first months a baby is fed on a purely liquid diet of milk with some water and fruit juice. At about five or six months of age she starts to need more food and is introduced to solid foods. This is the beginning of weaning. For several months she will continue both milk and solid food. Gradually the amount and variety of solid foods she is fed will be increased and the amount of milk she drinks will be reduced.

Weaning foods can be prepared by adapting family meals. In addition, bought packets and tins of weaning foods can be used. When giving the baby solid foods there are certain things to remember.

1 She needs the correct nutrients in the right quantities. No sugar should be added to the baby's food as it may make her too fat. Prepared baby foods contain some sugar anyhow. Salt should not be added as the baby's body may not be able to get rid of it and it could cause damage to the kidneys.

2 A baby up to about ten months of age does not have enough teeth for biting. She will be even older before she has teeth to chew. So her food has to be sieved, mashed or blended so that she can swallow it easily.

3 Meal times can be happy, but the family has to be patient. When she first tastes a new food a baby may spit it out and refuse to take any more. This can be upsetting if the dish has been specially prepared. However, forcing a baby to eat something she does not like will only make matters worse.

When a baby is about eight or nine months old she enjoys trying to feed herself. At first she may not be very successful and will make a mess. She will start eating using her fingers. Later on she will be able to hold and control a small spoon. She is still learning and cannot feed herself properly yet. She needs her mother to spoon most of the food into her mouth. A baby or young child may choke on a piece of food. So a responsible person has to be with her while she is feeding herself.

## 2 Activity, exercise and play

Babies and young children are very active and often roll, crawl, walk or run for the sheer pleasure of moving. Activity exercises the body and helps to strengthen the muscles. In the same way physical activities like swimming, rock-climbing, hockey and dancing

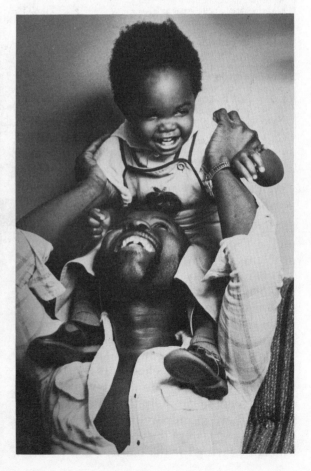

help to develop strong muscles and healthy bodies in teenagers and adults.

In the first few months a baby enjoys kicking and waving her arms. By eight or nine months even a baby who does not crawl can move about the floor to a surprising extent by rolling. Later she will start pulling herself up to stand, and try to walk. This kind of activity is natural for a child and gives her the chance to learn more about the world she lives in. By moving around, the child learns about the space surrounding her and the relationship between her own body and other objects. When moving her body the child is practising co-ordinating and controlling her movements so that they become smoother and less clumsy. A toddler frequently bumps into things because she is still learning about the space around her and because she does not have full control over her body.

As the child moves about she discovers what she can do with her body. The more she practises, the more skilled she becomes. She gains self-confidence and becomes more in-

dependent. A young child particularly enjoys her parents joining in with some rough and tumble, chasing or racing.

Children of three and four years are better able to control their movements and are more confident than the baby or toddler. They can be very adventurous and enjoy using some of the large climbing equipment usually available in nursery schools and playgroups. They also enjoy the delicate movements needed to handle building bricks, construction toys, simple jigsaw puzzles, sewing and carpentry (see physical play p. 121).

## 3 Sleep and rest

Most young babies need a great deal of sleep. A newborn baby sleeps for about fifteen to eighteen hours each day and is awake for no longer than about two hours at a time. As she gets older less time will be spent sleeping. Most toddlers sleep for about twelve hours each day.

A child who does not get enough sleep will be affected in the same way as an overtired teenager or adult. She will have difficulty concentrating and become bad tempered and unco-operative. But the child does not know that she is tired and needs to rest. The parent has to recognise when the child is beginning to tire. Before being put to bed the child may have to be calmed down by an adult talking, singing or reading to her.

## 4 Warmth

Some of the internal functions of the body, like digestion and release of energy from food, only take place if the body is at the correct temperature. If the body becomes too cold or too hot these processes will not take place and the person may die. In cold winters we hear sad stories of elderly people or babies dying of hypothermia when their bodies become too cold.

Normally the human body is kept at a constant temperature of 98.4°F or 37°C. Older children and adults are able to keep their bodies at the correct temperature without thinking about it much. However, the mechanism that keeps the body at the right temperature is not fully developed until about seven years of age. Babies and young children lose body heat quickly in cold conditions and can become overheated when it is hot. So their parents have to protect them against variations in temperature.

In cold weather a baby has to be kept warm and dressed in warm clothes. When the weather is hot she needs to be kept cool and dressed lightly. It is important to keep a baby warm when she is asleep. A newborn baby should sleep in a room heated to 70°F or 44°C, while an older baby should sleep in a room at 65°F or 41°C.

## 5  Health care

Before birth a foetus is in a sterile environment. The mother's womb is completely free of bacteria and viruses. When she is born she enters a world full of bacteria and viruses. Some of them do her no harm or may even be helpful. Others are harmful and can make her ill. A child who is frequently ill may not grow as rapidly as she should because her body's resources are taken up in fighting infection. So good health care to prevent and treat infections is important for physical development.

A child's health care is not only the responsibility of nurses and doctors. They can give help and advice, but most of the health care is provided by the child's parents. They can help prevent infection by:

### 1 Keeping the child clean

Dirty teeth, hands, fingernails and bottoms are breeding grounds for bacteria which may cause illness. Adults and teenagers can keep themselves clean. However, babies and young children need other people to wash them and keep them clean. As they grow older children start to wash their own hands and faces and to go to the toilet on their own. It is fun and more grown up to do these things for themselves; it is the beginning of independence. However, an adult should be around to help and encourage.

### 2 Clean food

Eating food prepared in unhygienic conditions may also lead to illness. Unwashed hands and dirty cooking utensils can introduce infection. Food that is not properly cooked or old may be infected and cause food poisoning or sickness and diarrhoea. People who look after a baby have to make sure that her bottle is sterilised and the feed is clean and safe to drink. Care is also needed when preparing her solid foods.

### 3 Immunisations

Some serious illnesses can be prevented by immunisations given by a doctor. Immunisation is a very effective way of combating disease. Smallpox is a deadly infection that has been eradicated from the world by immunisation. Babies and young children can be protected against diphtheria, whooping cough, tetanus, polio and measles. Later on

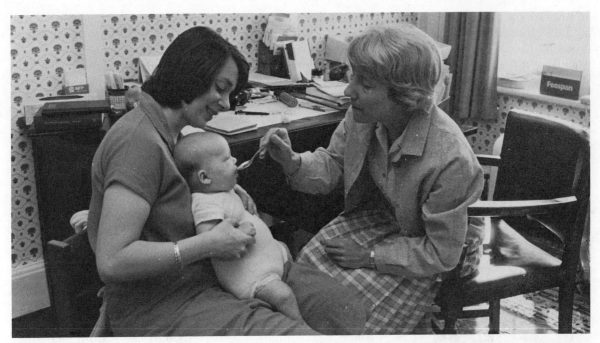

children can be immunised against tuberculosis and against German measles, which is particularly important for girls. Parents can provide health care by making sure their children receive all the immunisations. If a child is not immunised and catches one of these diseases he or she could become seriously ill and die.

If a baby or child does become ill it is important to consult a doctor. The doctor's advice should be followed carefully and medicines should be given according to instructions.

## 6 Protection from danger

The appalling fact about accidents is that they need never happen. Thousands of young children are accidentally killed or injured each year. Some injuries are so severe that a child is physically handicapped for the rest of her life. Road accidents are sadly very frequent. In 1980 117 children under five years of age were killed in road accidents in Britain.

The home is one of the most dangerous places for a child. In 1980 285 children under five years of age were killed in accidents in their homes in Britain. (Statistics from Royal Society for Prevention of Accidents.)

Accidents can be prevented. The first step in prevention is understanding why children are so often involved in accidents. When caring for children adults have to remember that:

1 Children are curious and adventurous. They see the world around them as a vast playground to be explored. Children enjoy physical activities like climbing, jumping and running and sometimes they become overconfident and have accidents.
2 Young children may not have learned that some things around them are dangerous. So they may not realise that their actions have harmful consequences.
3 Children have a very different view of the world from adults. The world does not look the same when you are three feet tall. (Sometimes a child may be able to see and attempt to get at objects that an adult has not even noticed.)
4 Children do not understand the world in the same way as adults. For example, they

are not as good as adults at judging the speed and distance of cars on the road.

5 A child may know what is dangerous and still have an accident. If she is caught up in a game she may forget to take care, and run across a road without looking for cars.

6 Some children may not really understand the rules of safety. Before crossing a road they may recite the Green Cross Code like a magic spell to protect them, but it is unlikely that they can apply such rules when they are young.

Children are not even safe in their own homes. The kitchen is particularly hazardous with a stove, hot kettles and saucepans, knives, cleaning materials such as bleach and soda crystals, and electric equipment. All fires are a source of danger, whether they are coal, gas, electric or paraffin. The staircase and banister can be a tempting climbing-frame for an active child. Serious accidents can occur in the bathroom — a small child can

drown in a few inches of water. The medicine chest contains medicines and pills that look attractive but can be dangerous.

Even toys may be dangerous. Not all manufacturers act responsibly and sometimes unsafe toys are sold in shops and on market stalls. The toys may have sharp edges that can cut. A small piece like the eye of a soft toy may be pulled off easily and a child may swallow or choke on it.

*Safety precautions*

1 Parents have to make sure the objects a child uses are safe. When making or buying equipment and toys for a baby or child it is important to think of possible dangers. For example she should not be able to climb out of her cot or playpen, and when sitting in a highchair or pushchair she should be held in with a harness. In Great Britain you can tell that a piece of equipment has been tested for safety when it has a British Standards Institute (B.S.I.) kite tag.

The Kitemark.

2 The child can be prevented from getting at dangerous places and objects. Fireguards, stair-gates and a garden gate to keep the child off the road are all very important. Chemicals, medicines, tools, scissors and knives should be kept out of reach or in a locked cupboard.

---

**Trace the picture at the top of page 93 into your book.**

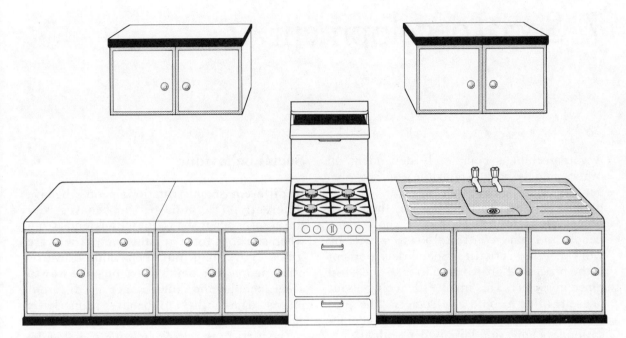

**Show on your drawing:**

**1 the correct position for a saucepan and kettle on the gas cooker**
**2 the safest place to store cleaning materials and detergents**

**3 a suitable place to store china and glass**
**4 a good storage place for: saucepans, wooden equipment, plastic dishes and mugs**

3 Children need to be supervised by an adult. At bathtime an adult should always stay close to a young child as she may slip and drown, or if she plays with the taps she may scald herself. If a child playing in a play-group or at home needs help, there is always an adult on hand. In Britain it is illegal to leave any children under the age of fourteen years alone in a house. This law was passed because children cannot be expected to look after themselves or take on responsibility for other children.

Each new skill brings new dangers. When a baby starts crawling, electric sockets and plugs and the staircase are more dangerous than when she was immobile. Later on she will start climbing and she will be likely to fall. Adults have to keep one step ahead of their children and make the house safe for them.

Babies and young children do not know about danger. But even very small children learn quickly from experience, and parents should accept a few bumps and scrapes as part of the learning process. They should by all means try to create a safe environment — but without being over-protective. As children grow older they start understanding explanations of why they should or should not do certain things.

**Collect information from newspapers, the Health Education Council, your local Health Education Department and child health clinic about the causes and prevention of accidents to children.**

**What points must you bear in mind when choosing: 1 a cot for a baby; 2 pyjamas for a small boy; 3 a toy; 4 fabric to make a child's nightdress?**

# 7  Social development

A young child is completely dependent on others and is not responsible for her own actions. Adults are independent of their parents and are responsible for their own homes and families. They may know many people and make contributions to society by work or other activities. Social development is the process of growing up to take one's full place in society. This involves learning about oneself, other people and society. The process of social development is called sociali-sation. Socialisation largely determines:

1  social behaviour
2  emotions
3  personality

## Social behaviour

In different social situations people behave differently. The same person behaves very differently when she is out with friends from when she goes for a job interview. There are 'rules' governing our behaviour towards other people, e.g. being courteous, the way to greet people and how to act in different places. The ability to behave properly is called a social skill.

The girls in the café are using social skills to order and pay for their refreshments. The teenager at the interview knows that she must behave in a certain kind of way if she wants to get the job.

People belong to social groups such as a family, church, school, club or group of friends. People who belong to the same social group often agree about social behaviour. For example, a 'gang' of school friends usually dress and behave in the same ways and like the same music and films. Their rules of behaviour are not written down. However, a person who dresses or behaves differently is often left out. He or she does not conform to the group.

Laws are rules of behaviour laid down by society. They control the way people behave towards each other. There are laws controlling such things as driving a car, wearing seat belts, buying and selling, stealing and murder. A person who breaks one of these laws behaves in an antisocial or *deviant* manner.

A baby is very helpless. She does not have social skills. She does not know about social rules or laws. She has a great deal to learn before taking her adult place in society. As a child grows older her social behaviour develops. She passes through the following stages:

1 the first relationships
2 early communication and independence
3 relationships outside home

## 1 *The first relationships*

Right from the beginning a baby has the equipment to respond to other people. There are her five senses (hearing, sight, touch, taste and smell) which she uses to receive information about the world. She also has a mind that tries to understand the world about her. From birth she responds to and is interested in other people. She does not have to be taught to be sociable. During the first months of life the baby is only concerned about herself. She is *egocentric*. If she is hungry, lonely, tired, cold or has a pain she wants to be comforted immediately. The signal she sends out to express her needs is her cry. In fact babies have different kinds of cry for different kinds of need. If her mother responds quickly the chances are she will cry less often. She is slowly learning to trust her mother. She knows she will come to her. These babies are often settled, more easily. On the other hand, when studied, mothers who allowed their babies to cry longer often had babies who cried loudly — just as you would shout louder in an emergency if nobody came. These babies were difficult to settle. They did not feel secure. As toddlers they did not want to be put down to explore and play.

In the first few months of life a baby learns

a great deal about other people. She learns by interacting with the people who care for her. From as young as three weeks of age she can recognise her mother's voice and respond to her. She can tell it apart from a strange woman's voice. At the the same age a breast-fed baby can recognise the smell of her own mother's breast. The bond with one particular person, usually her mother, is very important in the very beginning.

By the time she is two months old she joins in 'conversations' with another person. In these conversations the baby and her partner are influencing each other. They watch each other carefully. The baby's smiles, facial expressions and hand movements lead the adult to smile and talk to the baby. The baby then responds to the adult's changing facial expressions and voice. The adult needs to be patient, gentle and attentive. The conversations are great fun for both adult and baby. From about four or five months of age, babies enjoy playing 'social' games. They like fairly rough games with tickling and poking. They also enjoy gentle ones like peek-a-boo or singing games like pat-a-cake.

During the first year of life a baby forms emotional bonds with the people who care for her. These special relationships are known as *attachments*. A very young baby enjoys cuddles from anyone, but often if an eight-month-old is taken from her mother by a stranger she follows her with her eyes, then whimpers and cries. A baby also forms attachments to other people as well as her mother, e.g. her father, brother, sister, grandparents, or childminder. In all cases the baby forms an attachment to the people who spend time with her and play with her. It is these early safe relationships which will form the springboard for later ones. An older baby who has never been parted from her mother can become very upset when left with other people. Getting her used to being with other people helps her to begin trusting them.

## 2 Early communication and independence

By her first birthday a baby has started moving around by crawling or walking. She is also beginning to communicate. She may not know any words yet, but she can sometimes make other people understand what

A baby responding to its mother's changing facial expressions.

she wants by pointing, facial expressions and sounds. She can also understand some of the things her mother wants her to do. Soon she may even tease her by deliberately disobeying. Her ability to communicate improves gradually over the years as she starts talking and understanding other people better.

Babies are curious about the things that people do. They learn by joining in their activities and by imitating them. As a child learns she starts helping her parents to feed and dress her. Gradually she wants to do things for herself. She is becoming independent of her parents.

The young child starts being interested in life outside her home. She enjoys outings and meeting other children. Very young children do not play together. They watch or play alongside each other. As they grow older they appreciate the value of shared games. They learn a great deal about themselves and each other through playing together. Going regularly to a mother and toddler group, playgroup or nursery gives a child a chance to make friends with other children.

### 3 Relationships outside home

Going to a playgroup or nursery school is good preparation for starting school. The pre-school child has become more independent and self-confident. She is used to being away from her mother and can mix with other children. When she starts school her teacher is very important to her. She becomes fond of him or her and may correct her parents, telling them what her teacher has said. Her teacher may replace her mother as her 'model'. The time when a child starts school can be difficult for the mother. Her child is growing up and becoming more independent. She is no longer needed as much as she used to be, and may feel rejected. The relationship between mother and child is changing. However the child still depends on her parents a great deal and will need their help for many years to come.

As the child grows older her friends become increasingly important. She enjoys being in their company and may be a member of a gang or club. She learns through her friends. She finds out more about different homes and families. She discovers that the way her family does things is not the only way. The ideas her parents have are not the only ones. She will notice the differences between her family and those of her friends. Sometimes she will be embarrassed by her family. She may ask her mother not to wear a particular dress or not to mention a particular topic when her friends are present. She has become concerned about what her friends think of her family. Her horizons are widening and she is better able to understand other people's points of view.

### Backwards and forwards

Unlike other forms of development social development does not follow a steady pattern. A situation a child copes with one day might be beyond her the next. Much will depend upon the atmosphere or her environment and how she is feeling. She will find it difficult to be 'nice' when she is not feeling well.

Much social behaviour is learnt 'backwards'. She eats with her hands before she uses a spoon, she undresses herself before she manages to dress herself, she snatches toys before she learns to share. It will be these situations which provide adults around her with the opportunities to help her to develop social skills. She will need a lot of help and praise before she learns the 'rules'. Of course, if antisocial behaviour is ignored and encouraged she will never learn them.

## Emotions

Emotions are the moods and feelings people experience in the give-and-take of everyday life. They are a person's response to happenings around him or her. Examples of emotions are joy, anger, fear and sadness. It is usually possible to tell by a person's facial expression and behaviour what emotions he or she is feeling. We recognise emotions so we can treat other people appropriately, for example consoling someone who is sad or reassuring a person who is frightened. If people supress their emotions they can suffer from stress and insecurity. A baby needs to develop and learn about her emotions or she may not be able to cope with them when she grows up.

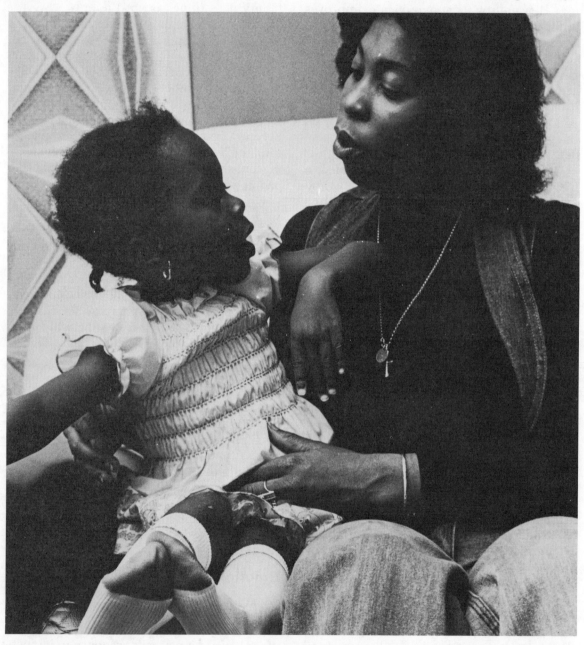

From an early age babies use emotions to communicate and they form emotional attachments to the people around them. As a child grows older she learns more about emotions through her experiences. She needs other people to help her in:

1 coping with her own strong emotions
2 understanding other people's emotions

## 1 Coping with strong emotions

Everyone experiences situations that give rise to strong feelings. It is natural to celebrate a joyful occasion like passing an examination or getting a new job. However some strong emotions have to be controlled. A person who gives vent to her anger may be destructive or hurt other people. Anger, resentment or jealousy can be difficult to control. However, it is easier if we can understand what is happening and see the other person's point of view. A young child is not able to do this. She has no control over her emotions. She does not understand them and may even be frightened by them.

As a child starts doing things for herself she experiences pleasure and pride. However, this independence may cause problems. When she is unable to do something she may become frustrated and angry. She may come into conflict with her parents. She wants to please her parents, and show that she loves them. But she also wants to please herself. She may become very angry and scream. She may throw herself on the floor and hold her breath. She may even be sick. These outbursts of anger are called temper tantrums. The child's parents must not be angry or reject her when she throws a temper tantrum. If they do, her anger and her fear will become more intense. She needs adults to respond calmly, hold her tightly, reassure her and distract her.

When a new baby arrives the older child may feel put out. She has had a great deal of her parents' attention and now she has to share it. She may feel jealous and dislike the baby.

In order to gain her parents' attention a child may copy the baby's behaviour. She may cry when she wants something instead of asking. She may talk using baby language and even expect her mother to feed her. This kind of behaviour is called *regression*. By acting like the baby, she hopes to become the centre of attention again. Parents need to be aware of how a new baby might affect the other members of the family and think of

**1 Why do you think Susan wants to hit her baby brother?**
**2 What do you think Susan's mother could do to help her overcome her jealous feelings?**

how they can deal with any problems.

As a child grows older, she needs help to understand and control her feelings. Parents and teachers have to explain what is happening. Each upset child needs someone to show they care about her and talk to her.

## 2 Understanding other people's emotions

A young child experiences hurt feelings when she is prevented from doing what she wants. However she does not understand that she can cause hurt feelings in others. She may snatch a toy from another child and play happily with it while the other child screams. She does not know that she has been the cause of the upset. It is up to the adult to link the two events for the child. Neither smacking nor allowing her to keep the toy will help her to learn from this experience. It is difficult for adults always to remember that a child may not understand what she has done. It is important that the adult does not destroy the confidence that the child may have found in a new relationship.

## Personality

Each person is unique. She is different from every other person, not only in her appearance but also in the way she thinks and reacts. Even identical twins are different from each other. An individual's 'personality' is displayed by the ways in which she reacts to situations in everyday life. Much of her behaviour is in turn affected by her personality.

---

**What do you do if you see your friends arguing? Do you:**

**1 ignore them and walk away?**
**2 stand and watch?**
**3 suggest they stop fighting as there are better ways to settle arguments?**
**4 get involved in the argument yourself?**

**What does your reaction tell you about your own personality?**

---

How personality is developed has been the subject of many studies. We know that one influence on our personality is the kind of relationship we have with our parents. That relationship begins to form from the moment we are born.

Margaret Mead was an anthropologist: she was interested in finding out why people in different kinds of societies had different personalities. The Arapesh and Mundugumor are people from two different kinds of societies who live in New Guinea, where Margaret Mead did her research.

The *Arapesh* are kind, gentle and sensitive people. Both the men and the women care fondly for their babies. During the first months of life the Arapesh baby has lots of cuddling. She is fed at the breast whenever she cries. The Arapesh children grow up with the same kind of personality as the adult members of their society.

The *Mundugumor* adults are competitive and aggressive. The Mundugumor baby is kept in a hard, solid basket. She cries for a long time before she is fed. The usual way of comforting a hungry or distressed baby is to scratch the outside of the hard basket. When she is fed she is held in a standing position facing the person feeding her. Close physical contact between a mother or father and their baby does not normally take place. Margaret Mead found that the Mundugumor baby also develops the same kind of personality as the adults in her society.

The first relationship a baby has is with the adult who feeds her. The baby who is fed as soon as she begins to feel hungry sees the adult as somebody who gives her nice feelings and takes away nasty feelings. If a baby is fed in a calm, unhurried and caring way she will develop good feelings. The baby is slowly beginning to feel that she matters. The person who feeds her will often be the person who goes to her when she cries.

This is the beginning of personality development. The way the adults respond to the baby will determine the kinds of personality traits she will develop. Her earliest experiences providing the basic ingredients which will shape her personality.

Here are some examples of personality characteristics:

| | |
|---|---|
| ambition | selfishness |
| apathy | kindness |
| creativity | jealousy |
| greed | humour |
| generosity | dishonesty |

**Which characteristics do you think are:**

**1 positive and more acceptable**
**2 negative and less acceptable**

**Give reasons for your answers.**

**Make a list of your own personality characteristics. Ask a friend to list them too. Compare the lists. Are the lists similar or different? Why do you think this is so?**

Even young babies are different from each other. Some are very active while others lie quietly, some cry a great deal, others are more contented. Mothers and fathers find that each of their children have different personalities from a very early age and they have to treat them differently. Active children need the chance to run about. Shy children have to get to know new people and places slowly. Some children are very interested in exploring toys. Others prefer spending time with people.

## Influences on social development

Social development is affected by genetic and environmental factors.

### Genetic influences

The genes a baby inherits from her parents will affect her social development. At birth babies are different from each other. Some are easy to comfort. Others are not. Some cuddle up to the person holding them, while others do not. These characteristics are probably affected by the child's genes. These earliest relationships will affect the baby's relationships with other people as she grows

older and may partly determine how later relationships work.

Little is known about the genetic influences on social development. The main reason for this is that it is very difficult to distinguish between genetic and environmental influences. For example, people may say that a child has inherited her personality or temper from one of her parents. However she may have learned to behave in this way by imitating her parents.

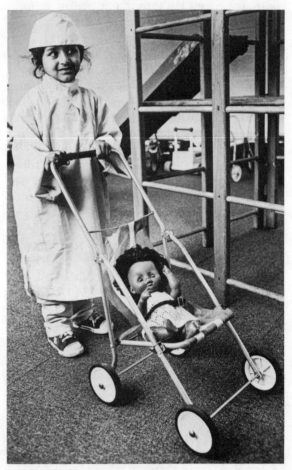

**Apart from imitating her mother what other factors could have influenced the child in this picture?**

### Environmental influences

A child's social development is affected by

her social environment. This is made up of all the people she comes into contact with. The way they treat her and their attitudes and ideas all affect her.

Parents and other people who care for children want to do their best for their charges. To help them, scientists have been studying what happens when children are treated in different ways. A psychologist called Dr Harlow wanted to find out what happened when a baby was deprived of her mother's care. He could not study human babies, so he studied Rhesus monkeys.

Dr Harlow put a baby monkey into a cage On its own. In the cage there were two wire models of monkeys. He called these models 'mother substitutes' because they had replaced the monkey's own mother. One mother substitute was covered with cloth and the other was left as bare wire. The wire model had a teat which provided milk. The cloth model had no milk. Dr Harlow studied many baby monkeys in this situation. He found that the baby monkeys cuddled up to the cloth-covered model. They only left it to go to the wire model to feed. One clever monkey managed to reach over to drink the milk without leaving the cloth model. Dr Harlow believed that they did this because they received some warmth and comfort from the cloth-covered model.

Later, Dr Harlow noticed that the baby monkeys did not feed as frequently. They sat hugging themselves and rocked backwards and forwards. They were not curious about their surroundings and did not play. When these monkeys grew up they did not mix with other adult monkeys. They did not care for their own babies but ignored or maltreated them, so Dr Harlow had to remove their babies from them.

In these experiments Dr Harlow put the monkeys into very extreme conditions. The monkeys which grew up to become such bad mothers had been reared without love and care. They had not had opportunities to develop a close relationship with a caring adult. They had been deprived. The effect was profound and lasting.

A few children have been found who have been extremely badly treated by their families. One, a girl called Genie, was fourteen years old when she was discovered. She had spent most of her life in one room. In the daytime her father strapped her onto a potty chair. She was only able to move her hands and feet. At night she was tied in a sleeping

bag and put into a cot. She rarely saw another person. Her father taught her brother to treat her like a wild dog. She was fed hurriedly three times a day. Her mouth was stuffed with soft food which she gradually swallowed. She had not learned to chew. When she was found she weighed only 4 stone 3 lb (22.9kg) and was only 4 ft 6 in. (137.16 cm) tall. She was very weak and could not stand or move about. Surprisingly she was curious about the hospital to which she was taken. She was hungry for human company and became attached to some of the hospital staff. After a great deal of care and help Genie learned to talk and started going to school. She made far better progress than anyone expected. However, she has not completely recovered from her lonely and deprived life.

If a child is totally deprived of a social environment, then social development is severely restricted. The close relationships which Genie was deprived of help a child to develop.

The vast majority of babies and young children are not so badly treated. However they are still influenced by their social environment. A child is affected by:

*1* parents
*2* other adults
*3* friends
*4* culture
*5* herself or himself

# 1 Parents

A child's parents affect her social behaviour, emotions and personality by their:

expectations
praise and criticism
consistency
example
explanations
acceptance or rejection

## Expectations

Every parent has expectations of his or her fine as long as the expectations are realistic. Not every child may have the ability or be interested in what the parents want. Parents forcing unrealistic expectations on children can make their lives miserable. The individual knows he or she can never achieve what they want. Sometimes parents' expectations are too low. They may not realise what the child can do and may dismiss her as a failure.

Occasionally parents notice talent in a young child, and through encouragement at an early age the child develops the skill rapidly. Mozart was a child prodigy. At a very early age he showed great musical talent and interest in music, and his father encouraged him. Mozart went on to become one of the greatest musical geniuses the world has ever known. If his father had not encouraged him when he was so young, Mozart might not have become as great as he did.

## Praise and criticism

Throughout life other people are commenting on what we do. An adult may be praised for doing a job well and even receive promotion or extra pay. We all enjoy being praised and probably do a job better because of it. Criticism can be very hurtful and discouraging, particularly to a young child. She is still learning. If she has not done well it may be the fault of the adults for not explaining properly. They might not be aware of her developmental stage of understanding. If the parent patiently helps and encourages, rather than loses his or her temper, the child is more likely to learn.

## Consistency

A young child needs to be treated in a consistent way by her parents. Some adults praise a child highly one day and the next day ignore or criticise everything she does. This can confuse and hurt the child. She does not know what to do to please her parents. She does not learn what behaviour is acceptable or unacceptable.

Sometimes each of her parents has different opinions about what the child should do. One parent may treat her in one way and the other in another way. This inconsistency between parents can also cause the child confusion. It also gives her the chance to play one parent off against the other.

### Example

A child learns from watching and being with other people. If people in her family behave in an aggressive way, she believes this is the way to treat people, and behaves aggressively too. A child brought up in a household where people treat each other with care and respect, learns to treat other people in the same way. (See 'How children learn — imitation' (p. 111).)

"Granny will fall over on these bricks. Pick them up immediately or I will smack you."

### Explanations

When she is very young a child accepts being told what to do. However, as she grows older and tries to understand more, she wants to know why. 'Because I say so' is no longer good enough. She needs her parents to explain. They can help her understand more about herself and other people.

### Acceptance or rejection

Parents show their acceptance by loving and helping their child in all situations. When a child has done something they do not approve of they say so. They may reject the child's act but not the child. A child who is accepted trusts other people and has no problem making friends. A child who is rejected probably feels insecure. She finds it difficult to trust other people and does not form relationships easily.

## 2 Other adults

In her life a child comes into contact with many adults. Some, like teachers, youth club

"We do not want Granny to fall over these bricks. She will hurt herself. I will help you. Let us see who can put most bricks in the box."

**In which situation do you think the child is more likely to co-operate? Why do you think so?**

leaders and church ministers, have authority over the child. These adults can all influence a child's social development. For example, some teachers and employers show particular attitudes to children of different cultural or ethnic groups. Asian children tend to do well at school partly because their teachers expect them to do well. Some teachers expect children of West Indian origins to do badly at academic work. As a result the children may have low expectations of themselves and may not do well at school. These are both examples of a self-fulfilling prophecy. This means that a person behaves in a particular way because other people expect her to behave in that way.

---

**Other adults influence a child in the same ways as her parents. Think of situations where a child's social development is affected by other adults' expectations; praise and criticism; consistency; example; explanations; acceptance or rejection.**

---

## 3 Friends

A child's friends are very important to her. Her parents and other adults are responsible for her. She has to respect their authority. However, with her friends a child has a more equal relationship. Friends can effect a child's social development. She may become more self-confident because her friends say she is good at sport or clever. Through her friends she can develop new interests and opinions.

---

**Think of situations in which a child will be affected by friends' expectations; praise and criticism; consistency; example; explanations; acceptance or rejection.**

---

## 4 Culture

This is made up of the values, attitudes, beliefs and behaviour of a group of people. Different groups of people or societies have different cultures. Americans have a different culture from the Chinese. They behave differently, e.g. they greet each other and show courtesy in different ways. They have different beliefs. China is a communist state that discourages people from following a religion. America is a democracy and a large proportion of the people go to church. These cultural differences affect a child's social development. As children grow up they learn to behave in fundamentally the same way as the adults in their culture. They come to hold similar attitudes and beliefs, although superfically they might react against them for a time.

In many British families the needs of the child are considered to be more important than the needs of the adults. Such families are called child-centred. Families may be child-centred in different ways, for example:

*Mary and Ted Smith* have a daughter. They try to meet her needs by doing things with her. They spend time talking, playing and comforting her. They feel it is important to give her opportunities for new experiences.

*Josie and Nick Johnson* have a daughter. They try to meet her needs by giving her all that the family can afford to buy. She has an extensive range of toys and many clothes. They feel it is important to try to give her everything that she asks for.

---

**The way a family meets a child's needs tells us something about their values.**

**What values do you think the Smiths and Johnsons have?**

**Do the families have different values?**

**How do you think their values influence the social development of their children?**

---

Some children grow up in a family which has a different cultural background from other families in the area. A child from a Welsh or Punjabi family living in a large English city is a member of a minority group. She has a different culture from the majority of people who live in that city. Young children are often unaware of the cultural and physical differences of their playmates. However, as they grow older these children begin to see themselves as different from other children. They may also be treated differently by other people.

## 5 Ourselves

Everyone has interests, ambitions, opinions and desires and these influence social development. For example, a child wanting to please the adults around her may dress neatly and remember to say 'Please' and 'Thank you'.

We all think we know ourselves. We know what we are like, what we can do and how we get on with other people. This is our idea of ourself, or our *self-concept*. A person's self-concept affects the way she relates to other people. For example, a child who feels confident will mix easily and enjoy playing with other children.

The way other people treat a person influences her self-concept. A child who has been given a lot of love feels that she matters. She has a better self-concept than a child who has been rejected. A rejected child will feel that she has little worth and matters to nobody. Our self-concept will influence the way we relate to other people.

Billy is four and a half. So far in his life nobody seems to have cared much about him. How do you think this may affect Billy's behaviour when he is a little older?

How may Billy behave towards the following?

1 his parents
2 his classmates in the infant school
3 his infant teacher

*Learning male and female roles*

Sarah and Jonathan look so similar it is impossible to tell which is which. However, by the time they are five years old everyone will know which is the girl and which the boy. By this age the children will have found out that people expect different kinds of behaviour from them. When Sarah is hurt while playing she may be cuddled and comforted. However when Jonathan is hurt he may be told not to cry but, 'Be brave, like a soldier.'

Knowing how boys and girls are expected to behave is learned in many ways. Children see their mothers and fathers behaving differently and doing different kinds of jobs. Children's books and television often show different behaviour for boys and girls. In fact, many children live with only one parent, who has to be both housewife and handyman at home. These days responsible people in the media are more careful about male and female stereotypes. But our society still encourages differences as the table shows.

**Look at advertisements, comics and magazines. In what kinds of situations do you frequently see girls, and boys?**

**Are the girls often dressed in particular colours?**

**Are the boys often dressed in particular colours?**

**Compare your findings with those in the table. Can you add to the table?**

| Situation | Girls | Boys |
|---|---|---|
| Clothing | Often dressed in pink | Often dressed in blue |
|  | Play clothes may be the same but best clothes are different | |
| Play and behaviour with friends | Rough behaviour discouraged<br>Expected to be gentle | Sometimes allowed to play rough<br>Gentle behaviour may be thought 'cissy' |
|  | Given dolls and toy domestic appliances<br>Play at 'women's work', e.g. mother and nurse | Given train sets and footballs<br>Play at 'men's work', e.g. train driver, father and spaceman |
|  | In an argument expected to leave the scene | Expected to fight back |
| At home | Encouraged to help mother | Encouraged to help father |
| Books and magazines | Often shown as being good with people | Often shown as being good with machines and science equipment |
|  | Depicted as being passive and romantic | Depicted as decision makers and involved in action |

**As shown in the table, boys and girls tend to be given different sorts of toys. In groups, discuss whether you think parents should encourage their children to play with the toys traditionally associated with the opposite sex.**

## Children with special needs

Most children grow up with no major problems. However some children do need special care at some time in their lives. Three of these groups are:

1 battered children
2 handicapped children
3 children in hospital

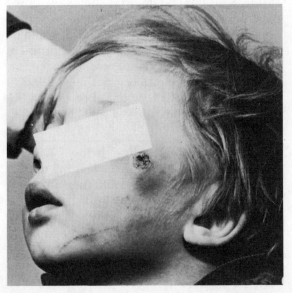

A battered child.

## Battered children

It is a sad fact that every year thousands of children are battered by their parents. Sometimes babies and children die from these attacks. Parents who batter their children come from all walks of life. They may be young and unemployed or older and comfortably off. However, studies show that there are similarities between parents who batter. Often they have been badly treated as children themselves. They are repeating the pattern of their own early life. They sometimes feel the baby does not love them. When the baby cries, soils or feeds messily they feel that he or she is being deliberately difficult. Often a crisis in the home causes the parent to start maltreating the baby. The crisis may be shortage of money, for example, or losing a job or home, or a breakdown in the marriage.

Parents maltreat their children in a variety of ways. They may be physically violent and beat, shake, burn or scald the child. Some parents neglect the physical needs of the child. They may not feed or clothe her properly or keep her clean and dry. Other parents cause emotional distress to their child. They may tell her they do not love her and cruelly tease her. Some parents may exercise so much control over what their children attempt to do, that they slow down their development.

Parents who maltreat their children can be helped. They should talk about their problem to the doctor, health visitor, social worker or, in Britain, to an officer of the N.S.P.C.C. (National Society for the Prevention of Cruelty to Children).

> **Read the case studies below, which describe the circumstances leading up to a child being badly hurt, and then answer the questions.**

*Henry and Susan* were professional people. Henry was a doctor, Susan worked full-time as a chemist in a large industrial plant. They had been married for six years before their first baby was born. It was a boy, Ian. Henry was delighted — 'When he grows up I want him to be a doctor,' he would say. The baby was beautiful. He had large brown eyes and a strong, healthy body.

Susan returned to work when Ian was three months old. He was looked after by a series of *au pairs*. Just after Ian started the nursery school, the head teacher asked if she could meet Sue and Henry. She was concerned because Ian had found difficulty in getting along with other children. He demanded the attention of his nursery teachers continuously. He behaved badly when he could not have his own way. He could not hold a pencil or use scissors. When he was given paints he splashed them on other children. Henry and Susan were embarrassed because they felt their son had let them down.

*Jocelyn* had a baby when she was nineteen. She had not married the father. Her mother looked after her baby, Elizabeth, and Jocelyn continued to work. When Elizabeth was two years old Jocelyn met Dick. He was three years younger than Jocelyn. Dick was a popular lad. He played in a group and was something of a heart-throb with the girls. Jocelyn and Dick married just six months after they met. The three of them moved into a brand new flat.

When Jocelyn asked Dick to help out he would say, 'I'm not really turned on to kids.' He had been an only child, and was resentful that Elizabeth took up so much of Jocelyn's time. He was even more alarmed when he discovered that he was expected to baby-sit when Jocelyn did the shopping on Saturday afternoons with her mother. Before he married, Dick had enjoyed watching a game of football on Saturday afternoon. The situation was made worse because Elizabeth usually screamed when her mother left her.

In each of the situations above a young child was severely battered.

**1 What kinds of feelings do you think Susan and Henry had which caused them to punish Ian after the visit to the school? Who do you think could have helped Henry and Susan?**

**2 Why do you think that Dick hit Elizabeth? Are there solutions to this problem?**

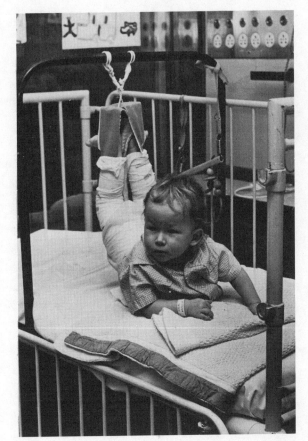
A child in hospital.

## Handicapped children

Sadly, many children are deaf, blind or handicapped physically or mentally. Some children are born handicapped. Others become handicapped as the result of an illness or accident. Handicapped children have the same social and physical needs as other children. Because of their handicaps they also have special needs. They may need special medical attention. They may need training to help them overcome their handicaps. Blind children are taught to read and write and to move about and do things without having accidents. Deaf children are taught to speak and to lipread. Children with physical handicaps are helped to be more independent. Children with a mental handicap, like Down's Syndrome, are taught as much as possible about their world and how to do things for themselves. Not all handicapped children need to go to special schools. Many go to ordinary schools.

Parents of handicapped children can become very upset and may feel guilty about their child's handicap. They can get help in coping with a handicapped child from doctors, health visitors and social workers. There are also voluntary organisations with special interests in children with handicaps, e.g. Royal National Institute for the Blind, Spastics Society, Mencap.

## Children in hospital

If a child has to go to hospital it is very important that the mother or some close relation should stay with him or her for as much time as possible. This can cause difficulties at work or with other children at home, but it is the one in hospital whose need is greatest.

Although small children are generally good at accepting what happens to them, even if it includes pain, they are very frightened if they cannot be understood by the people around them. A mother can act as a go-between — she has the time to explain what is going to happen to the child and also to interpret the child's needs to the medical staff. Most hospitals now make it possible for parents to stay close to their children if they are needed, as studies have shown that children suffer far less anxiety in hospital if they are not left on their own, and return to life at home far more easily. At one time it was thought that visits from parents only upset children and that they were quieter if the parents kept away. In fact a child who is 'quiet' in this way is usually deeply distressed and frightened.

Parents who know their toddler or pre-school child will have to stay in hospital can prepare them for it in quite a positive way. After all, a children's ward is an exciting place to be and most of the time is spent getting better. Children can play at doctors and nurses and wear masks and hats like they do in operating theatres. There are plenty of books about hospital to look at. Packing a hospital case can be quite fun — it should certainly include a favourite teddy or comfort rag. Children need to be reassured that they will come home again soon, perhaps by pointing out which flowers will be in bloom when they come back.

A child who has just come out of hospital usually demands a lot of attention and is very likely to regress in some way. She may want to be fed, or come into her parents' bed every night. She has been away and feels left out. The more secure and loved she is made to feel the more quickly this stage passes.

# 8 Learning and the development of intelligence

## Learning

From the moment that a baby is born she begins to learn. Learning means acquiring knowledge and skills by experience, studying, or by being taught. For example many children learn to ride a bicycle by experience. They are taught table manners and study to improve their knowledge. Often they learn by a combination of these methods.

### How children learn

Children learn by:

1 praise and encouragement
2 punishment
3 experiencing success
4 discovery
5 imitation

### 1 Praise and encouragement

Children frequently learn because they are rewarded for doing something in a particular way. Praise and encouragement are important rewards. A school pupil will be likely to try harder if she has received a good mark and an encouraging comment for a piece of work. Praise and encouragement are called *positive reinforcement.*

### 2 Punishment

In order to discourage certain behaviour some form of punishment may be used. For instance a teacher may send a child to stand outside the classroom door for a few minutes as a punishment for talking during a lesson. Punishment is called *negative reinforcement.*

### 3 Experiencing success

Some psychologists believe that experiencing success is an important reward that helps learning. If a child is to experience success the tasks set for him or her must not be too difficult. They must be appropriate to the age and ability of the child. A two-year-old cannot be expected to have good table manners and a four-year-old is unlikely to be able to read the daily newspaper.

### 4 Discovery

While playing, children sometimes discover something they did not know before. When a child puts a cork and a pebble into water she quickly finds out that a cork floats and a pebble sinks. Science lessons are a good example of discovery learning.

### 5 Imitation

When a young child plays she is likely to do things that her mother or father do. She may imitate exactly the words and gestures her mother or father uses.

## Development of intelligence

Intelligence determines the level at which we learn and think. As a child grows up she progresses through stages in her ability to learn and think. Her intelligence changes and develops.

A newborn baby only sucks, cries and moves her body. She does not show much intelligence. However, she starts learning straight away. When she is two or three months old she is fascinated by moving objects. Soon she will start hitting the

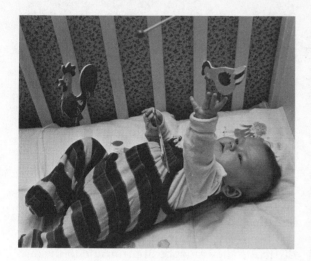

mobiles that hang from her cot and chuckle as she watches them swing. She develops an intense interest in the feel of things. She explores objects by handling them and putting them to her mouth. This preoccupation with the sight and feel of objects marks the earliest steps in the child's learning and is very important in her first year.

When an eight-month-old baby drops a toy over the side of her pram she makes no attempt to look for it. She seems to think that it has gone. Also at this age, if the baby is trying to get a toy and another object is in the way she just pulls harder at the toy. She does not realise that if she moved the obstructing object she could easily get the toy. Her ability to think has not developed enough to work this out. By the time she is one year old the baby will be able to solve this problem. If she drops a toy over the side of her cot she will also look for it.

Between twelve and eighteen months children become interested in the uses of objects. For example the actions they use playing with a toy telephone are similar to those of adults. They start to pretend to do things like cooking, drinking and eating. They pretend to 'feed' their dolls. This shows that they are beginning to understand more about the things that people do.

Adults think using abstract ideas. For example their ideas about good and evil are general principles and do not describe any particular person or event. A young child's thought is not abstract like an adult's. Her thought is concrete. This means that she understands the world in terms of what she sees and does. Her ideas of good and evil are descriptions of her own experiences. To be good means obeying parents and not hurting another person.

It is not until a child is about seven years old that she begins to think logically. However it will be many years before her thinking is as logical as an adult's. At seven years of age a child still cannot understand abstract ideas. She still only really understands concrete things. Mathematics involves abstract ideas and logic. It is for this reason that in the first years at school children use counters to help them study mathematics. For most people the ability to think in an abstract and logical way does not develop until the late teenage years.

## Concepts

As a person learns he or she forms concepts. A concept is an idea about objects or events. People use concepts to identify objects that are similar in some way. For example some objects are grouped together because they are the same colour or shape. People also form concepts about size, speed, distance and numbers and they use concepts to try to understand the world around them.

The fact that our minds form concepts helps us to learn, think and remember.

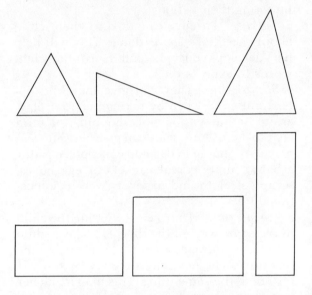

Here are six different shapes. Three of the shapes have three sides and three of them have four sides. You will immediately recognise them as being triangles and rectangles. Once you have recognised that these are three triangles and three rectangles, remembering the shapes becomes easier. Your brain has less information to store. This is because your brain only has to cope with the variations on two basic shapes rather than dealing with six quite different pieces of information.

---

**Try to work out how you would describe each of these shapes if you were not allowed to use the words 'triangle' and 'rectangle'.**

---

The development of intelligence involves changes in concepts. With new experiences a child's concepts become more complex. A five-month-old baby can focus her eyes on a nearby object and reach out and touch it. She is beginning to judge distances. She has formed a concept of distance. However, this concept is very simple. It will take many years full of experiences before she has a fully developed concept of distance. This is one of the reasons why it is dangerous to let young children out on the street on their own. In order to cross the road safely it is necessary to judge:

1 how far away the cars are
2 how long it will take the cars to reach the point in the road at which we are standing
3 how long it will take to cross the road

In order to make the correct decision all this information has to be dealt with simultaneously and quickly.

---

**Make a list of the concepts that a child could learn when playing with this toy. Make up a game that would help a young child learn the concept of colour.**

---

## Factors influencing learning and intelligence

The way that people learn and think is studied by psychologists. There are two views about why some people learn more easily or are more intelligent than others:

1 Intelligence is innate — this means that the ability to learn and think is determined by the genes a person inherits. The surroundings make no difference.

2 Intelligence is the result of experience — this means that some people learn more because of their opportunities and experiences.

Psychologists are divided on this issue. Some hold the first view, while others disagree and believe the second to be true. There are other psychologists who say that both a person's genes and experiences influence his or her intelligence. A child may have the genetic potential to be good at mathematics. But in order to fulfil this potential she needs the right experiences. She will be helped if her parents have a positive attitude to the subject and encourage her. She also needs to be taught mathematics well at school.

A person's ability to learn is also influenced by other factors. The brain is the organ of the body concerned with learning. If the brain is severely damaged by injury or illness, learning will slow down and may even stop. A person's interests and personality affect his or her ability to learn. For example, patience, concentration, a good memory and determination to succeed all help learning.

## How parents can help children learn

By the time they start school children have already learned a great deal. The words they use tell us how much they know. Before starting school most children can name a wide variety of objects. They also know the names of colours, shapes, sizes and some numbers. This knowledge helps them at school. For example, recognising different shapes helps them to learn to read and write.

Parents are the child's first teachers. They are responsible for her learning in the pre-school years. They can help her learn through:

1 encouragement
2 showing
3 talking
4 stimulating
5 consistency

*1 Encouragement* By their attitude and interest parents can encourage a child's desire to understand the world around her.

*2 Showing* Parents can show their child how to do things so that she can learn by imitating their actions.

*3 Talking* Parents can talk to their child about the things she is doing. This will help her develop concepts and learn the right words to express them.

*4 Stimulating* They can give the child opportunities to learn by taking her to a play-group or nursery school, shopping, or on a visit to a museum. They can give her things to play with that help develop concepts, e.g. (for a baby) empty cereal packets or egg boxes, scraps of cloth and paper as well as educational toys.

*5 Consistency* This means treating the child in the same way all the time. One day a child may be encouraged to build a cave using the furniture. The next day she may be told off for doing the same thing. This may make her uncertain about her parents' attitude and may inhibit her.

**What can each of these children learn? How could some of them be helped to improve their opportunities for learning?**

## Play

*Reasons for play*

Play includes a variety of activities. It can be noisy and active or quiet and serious. It can involve being alone or with other people. People of all ages play for amusement, exercise or to help them relax. It helps divert them from the physical and mental demands of their home, family and job.

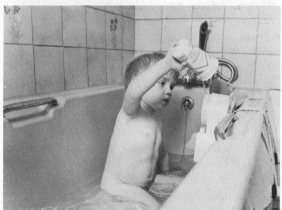

skills at different tasks and experience satisfaction at their success. For children a great deal of play is work.

*Development of play*

At different ages babies and children play in different ways. As a child grows older her play becomes more complicated. The way she plays changes with the development of her social behaviour, intelligence, language and ability to move. Here is a description of the play of children at different ages. It is important to remember that children do not all develop at the same rate and there will be variations in the age at which some stages are reached.

*The first six months*   Babies aged six weeks and older enjoy playing with other people. They watch and respond when a person talks and smiles at them. Their early conversations are their first social play.

From about two months of age a baby takes a great interest in her body. She discovers her feet, hands, toes and fingers. The baby takes great delight in being naked. When lying naked on a towel in a safe place, she kicks and chuckles with delight at her freedom of movement.

Young babies are interested in objects. They find brightly coloured, moving, rattling toys particularly attractive. Between birth and two months babies are very shortsighted and in order for them to focus, objects have to be held eight to ten inches (20 to 25 cm) from their eyes.

While people of all ages play it is the young who play most of all. Children play a great deal of the time and they seem to have great fun. Much of what adults call play is serious activity for children. It is through play that they learn. A child finds out about objects and what happens if she performs particular actions on them. She also learns about other people, how to get on with them and about their feelings. While playing, children develop

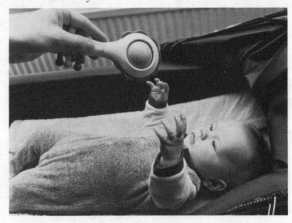

This four-month-old baby is looking at the rattle. At first she hit it by accident and was interested when it moved and made a noise. Soon she learned that she was making it move and rattle when she hit it. This helped her learn about the connection between what her eyes see and what her hands do. This is called hand and eye co-ordination. From four to five months of age babies become increasingly curious about objects and start grasping and holding them. They also use their mouths to feel and explore. So it is important that very small or sharp objects are not given to a baby.

For the first six months a baby's interest is in the weight, colour, shape and feel of objects. She cannot make them work or make up games. She is only able to concentrate for short periods and can only attend to one object at a time. If she has one toy and is then offered a second one, she will drop the first and take the second. The first toy will be completely forgotten. Even a young baby becomes bored and irritable if she has nothing to interest her or if her toys are always the same. Frequently changing her toys prevents her from becoming bored.

**Why do you think these games give so much pleasure?**

**Make a collection of household objects suitable for a baby aged nought to six months to look at, touch, hit, hold and suck. Remember that they must not have sharp edges or be small enough to swallow.**

*Six to twelve months* At this stage a baby enjoys repetitive games such as peek-a-boo, pat-a-cake and round and round the garden. She soon starts recognising the game by the song or rhyme, and smiles and laughs at the actions.

Between six and twelve months there are many changes in the baby's ability to move. She starts to sit up, roll, crawl and stand. She enjoys her new skills and often moves for the sheer joy of doing so. She also moves about to explore and play with toys.

At about nine months she starts to be able to attend to two objects at the same time. She

enjoys hitting objects together and filling a container with objects and then tipping them out again. She is interested to know what happens to a toy when she drops it and looks to see where it has fallen. She is also able to find an object that has been hidden under a cloth.

*One to two-and-a-half years*  Most children are able to walk by the time they are fifteen months. As the child's ability to move develops she becomes interested in toys that move. She enjoys pushing a cart, pulling a train and chasing a ball. She also tries to find out more about what she can do with her body. As she gains confidence she tries climbing, jumping and running. Remember, though, that children develop at different rates and it does not mean there is anything wrong with a child who is not walking at fifteen months.

At this age children are interested in everyday activities like cooking, cleaning and shopping. They try to join in with the things adults are doing and imitate their actions. They also start imaginative play: e.g. they feed their dolls and put them to bed.

In this period children learn more about objects. They touch, shake, squeeze and drop them to see what happens. They also combine objects in different ways, e.g. stacking bricks in a tower and later building a simple house or car using construction toys.

A small child soon becomes bored and loses interest if she is left alone to play. She needs someone to provide her with a variety of play materials. It takes a great deal of patience and planning for parents to give the child the amount of attention that she demands.

*Two-and-a-half to seven years*  Children of these ages still enjoy the sorts of play activities they enjoyed earlier. However their play gradually becomes more sophisticated and complicated. They become more inventive and imaginative as they bring in all sorts of ideas and experiences. They adapt everyday objects to fit in with their play; a bowl becomes a hat and a cardigan a doll's blanket.

As their knowledge about the world increases, their drawings and constructions begin to represent objects and often have a surprising amount of detail. They also enjoy jigsaws and other puzzles.

At about two-and-a-half years children begin to play with other children, i.e. they join in social or co-operative play. As they become older they start playing games with simple rules, like hide-and-seek and tag. Then they become more interested in the rules and are concerned that everyone should follow them correctly. As their language develops they start playing with words and try telling jokes and riddles. However, younger children do not always understand the riddle or joke and may tell a muddled version.

Frequently a small child will want an adult to play with her. She will need an adult to look for her when she hides, to fill her bucket with water or to demonstrate the possibilities of an object or toy. This gives the adult the opportunity to have fun with the child and also extend her play by introducing new ideas.

**Study this photograph of a child playing in the bath. What is this child learning when playing with water?**

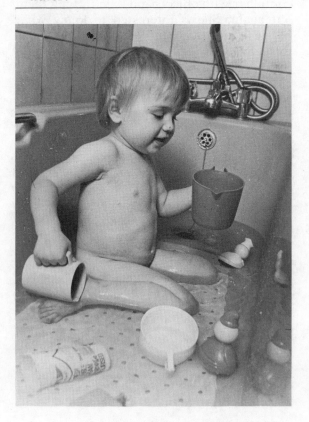

**Some teenagers and adults interfere in a child's play. They tell her what to do and take over the game. Do you think this is desirable or undesirable? What are the reasons for your answer?**

As they grow older, children become more independent in their play. However, a child cannot be told to go away and play. She still needs someone to provide her with the space, toys and play materials and she still needs supervision.

## Playing alone and with others

Children can become involved in:

1  solitary play
2  parallel play
3  social or co-operative play

*1  Solitary play*

Sometimes a child plays on her own, paying no attention to other children around her.

People of all ages, including young babies, at times become involved in solitary play.

*2  Parallel play*

At first a child will be unable to share her toys and co-operate in games with another child. She will be happy to play alongside the other child, each with their own toys.

*3  Social or co-operative play*

Babies enjoy playing games with their parents. This is the earliest form of social play. However, the baby and parent are not equal partners in the game. It is largely up to the parent to keep the game going.

It is not until the child is about two-and-a half years old that she is able to play with another child. They can pretend to be mothers and fathers, or together build a castle out of bricks. Playing together, children start to learn about sharing, helping and being tolerant. The beginning of co-operative play marks a change in the child's social behaviour. She is beginning to understand that other children experience emotions and feel pain, as she does. She still has a great deal to learn about getting on with other children, and there are frequently tears and squabbles that have to be sorted out by an adult.

## Types of play

Playgroups and nursery schools have materials for a wide variety of play activities. These are carefully planned to help children develop particular skills and knowledge. There are provisions for the following types of play:

1 discovery
2 creative
3 imaginative
4 physical

### 1 Discovery play

Some play materials can help a child's intellectual development. By handling objects and materials in different ways she can gain knowledge and develop concepts.

Sally is finding out about modelling and making shapes with dough.

### 2 Creative play

Through creative play a child develops her artistic skills and learns about shapes and colour. As her knowledge of the world

increases, she finds new ways of representing places and people.

Most three-year-olds are not yet able to draw recognisable objects, but can control their crayons to make circles and vertical lines.

### 3 Imaginative play

This type of play is sometimes called pretend, make-believe or fantasy play. Children often imagine they are someone else or in another place. This kind of play helps to widen their understanding of the world. Pretending to be someone else helps them develop sympathy for other people's feelings. It can also help them understand the world around them and the kinds of work that people do.

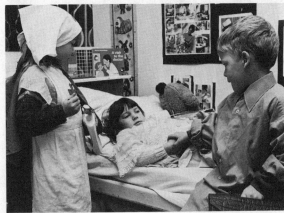

Hannah, Susan and Jonathan are pretending to be a nurse, a patient and a doctor. Perhaps one of them has recently been in hospital or is going into one and they are acting out their fears.

### 4 Physical play

Through physical play a child learns more about what her body can do. She develops control of her muscles. She becomes more skilful at co-ordinating the different parts of her body, e.g. her arms and legs in climbing and her hands and eyes in catching a ball.

**Complete this chart to show other
examples of each type of play.
Children can play in any of these ways,
alone or with other children. For each
type of play give examples of solitary
and social play.**

| Type of play | Example of play and play materials required | What the child is finding out |
| --- | --- | --- |
| **Discovery** | | |
| solitary | | |
| social | | |
| **Creative** | | |
| solitary | | |
| social | | |
| **Imaginative** | | |
| solitary | | |
| social | | |
| **Physical** | | |
| solitary | | |
| social | | |

You will find out more about the importance of play in Chapter 9.

# 9 Language

## Human communication

A large part of our lives is spent conveying information and in social interaction. This is called communication. The most important form of human communication is language. This is usually spoken or written. Many deaf people use another form of language — sign language. We use language in all our everyday activities, e.g. to get on with other people and in our work. Through language we can express our feelings, pass on information, ask questions and share views.

There are other forms of communication besides language. For example the baby's earliest communication does not involve language. She communicates distress by crying and pleasure by smiling.

**This is William. What can we tell about how William is feeling just by looking at this photograph? Make a list of methods of communication that do not use language. These forms of communication are called non-verbal communication.**

## Language development

To learn to speak, a child needs the right experiences. She has to be talked to, listened to and her questions answered. She needs a variety of experiences so that she will have something to talk about. If children are never spoken to they do not learn to speak. There are accounts of human tragedies that show this. Sometimes children have been kept isolated from other people. It is thought that some have been reared by wild animals. When found, these children have not been able to make human sounds.

This is Jane, who is three years old. She can now speak in simple sentences. Her language

development went through the same stages as that of most other children. These stages are:

1 babbling
2 single words
3 joining words together

As with all other aspects of human development it is not possible to predict exactly the age at which each stage is reached. The development of language involves not only making sounds and speaking words, but also understanding what other people say.

## 1 Babbling

When Jane was five weeks old she started making cooing and gurgling sounds. These early sounds are called babbling. Over the following months she spent a lot of time experimenting with sounds and discovering what her voice could do. She did this most often when she was happy and contented. Although she made a variety of sounds they did not have any particular meaning. Her babbling increased until it reached a peak between nine and twelve months.

Jane's parents spent a lot of time talking to her even though she was not able to use words herself. Jane could sense her mother's feelings by the tone of her voice. The way that her mother looked at her and talked to her were very important ways of communicating her love and care. When Jane made babbling sounds her parents listened and then replied.

A baby understands words before she says them herself. She listens to other people speaking and watches what they are doing. This way she learns what they mean. For language development it is more important to listen and understand than just to imitate words. When talking to Jane her parents used many actions and gestures. These helped Jane understand them when they said things like, 'Up you come!' and 'Down the stairs!'

## 2 Single words

Shortly after her first birthday Jane began to say her first words. She had begun to grasp the idea of using a particular sound to refer to a particular object. Within a few weeks she was using several words associated with everyday experiences. Her first words were 'Dada', 'duck' and 'bikit' (for biscuit).

For several months young children say only single words. They do not join words together. These single words are sometimes called one-word sentences. This is because a young child uses one word to try to express what an adult says in a whole sentence. Jane's mother learned to interpret what Jane meant when she said 'Dada'. She might mean:

'Daddy has gone out.'
'Daddy is coming home.'
'Daddy pick me up.'

To understand each other both Jane and her parents relied on what was happening at the time as well as listening to the actual words spoken.

Jane's parents talked to her about the things she was doing and interested in. They talked simply and clearly to help her understand. In this way she learned more words.

## 3 Joining words together

Once Jane knew a selection of single words she began to join two words together. She said things like 'Daddy gone', 'Mine milk' and 'Coat on'. She spoke using the essential words to convey her meaning. Sometimes she arranged the words in different ways to mean different things. When her mother took Jane's shoes off, Jane would say, 'Shoes off'. When Jane wanted to take her shoes off herself she would say, 'Off shoes'.

For some time Jane was not able to speak using correct English. She could not speak grammatically. Most English words are made into the plural by adding the letter 's' at the end, e.g. 'sock' becomes 'socks' and 'dog' becomes 'dogs'. Jane learned this rule and formed plurals correctly. However, sometimes she mistakenly applied this rule and said 'mouses' instead of 'mice' and 'sheeps' instead of 'sheep'.

Jane's parents helped by talking to her correctly and using complete sentences. They would say: 'I will help you put on your shoes and coat. Then we shall go to the park and feed the ducks,' rather than: 'Mummy'll put your coatee on and then we'll feed the duckies.'

Using the correct form gave Jane a good example. It showed her how to express her meanings clearly and correctly. Even though Jane used her own form of language her parents always used the correct form. When Jane fell down and said, 'Knee hurted fall down', her mother comforted her and said 'Have you fallen down and hurt your knee?'

Before she could start speaking in sentences Jane had to learn a great deal. She still makes mistakes and has more to learn. She will continue learning about language and how to express herself during her school years. Her parents will still play an important part in her language development.

## Widening language

A child's language can be widened by a variety of language experiences: 1 conversations; 2 books and stories; 3 rhymes and songs; 4 television and radio.

### 1 Conversations

A child's language can be expanded by listening, talking and answering questions. A child is more likely to want to talk if she has something to talk about. Visits to the park, shops, seaside or friends open up a whole range of experiences and vocabulary.

What a lot Elaine will have to tell Mummy about the ducks in the park.

If Mary spends all day like this she will have nothing to tell Daddy when he gets home.

**A bus journey is a good time to listen to the chatter that takes place between a mother and her young child. Study these two conversations carefully:**

| | |
|---|---|
| *Small boy* | 'Look car.' |
| *Mother* | 'Oh yes, there is a red car. It is like Daddy's car.' |
| *Small boy* | 'Daddy's car, Daddy's car.' |
| *Mother* | 'No it isn't Daddy's car, but Daddy has a red car that looks just the same.' |
| *Small boy* | 'Daddy gone.' |
| *Mother* | 'Yes, Daddy has gone to work. You waved him off after you had your breakfast.' |

| | |
|---|---|
| *Small boy* | 'Pieceman, piecemen.' |
| *Mother* | 'That is the policeman. He's directing the lorries and cars.' |
| *Small girl* | 'Where's Daddy?' |
| *Mother* | 'I've told you he's gone to work.' |
| *Small girl* | 'Where's Daddy?' |
| *Mother* | 'Be quiet. I've told you where he's gone.' |
| *Small girl* | 'Daddy's gone.' |
| *Mother* | 'Yes, Daddy's gone.' |
| *Small girl* | 'Where's Daddy?' |

**Which mother is helping her child's language to improve? How is she helping her child more than the other mother?**

## 2 Books and stories

Books and stories are an important part of a child's life. Even a young baby enjoys looking at picture books. The first book that a small child enjoys usually has just one large bold picture on each page.

If the pages are made of thick paper or cardboard the child can help turn them. She will soon be able to recognise pictures of objects that are within her experience, such as a teddy bear, cup, spoon and milk. Photographs are particularly good.

Later on the child will enjoy story books that have bright, colourful and simple pictures with only a few words on each page.

As the child gets older she will not need so many pictures to keep her attention. When being read to it is important that a child is sitting comfortably and can see the pictures. The child soon becomes bored if the story is read in a dull monotone. It is far more interesting when the reader puts expression into his or her voice and uses different voices for different characters.

Books help to widen a child's range of experiences. She is not likely to come across an elephant while out shopping, and city children may not know much about the seashore. However, through books they can find out about such things. Books and stories can help a child to cope with difficult emotional experiences. Stories about a visit to the dentist or a stay in hospital can help a child come to terms with her fear of dentists and hospitals.

Infant teachers often find that children who learn to read early have books at home, are read to regularly and are members of a library. Nearly all public libraries have a children's section with librarians specially trained to help choose books for children. In many libraries there are regular story times when someone reads or tells a story to a group of children.

## 3 Rhymes and songs

Children particularly enjoy nursery rhymes and songs. They like the sounds of the rhyming words and are soon able to remember them and join in. Some rhymes involve the child in some form of action. Before the child is able to memorise all of the words she will enjoy joining in with the actions.

---

**Make a list of all the action songs and nursery rhymes you can remember.**

---

## 4 Television and radio

Radio and television can play an important part in expanding children's language. If the television or radio is permanently turned on the child will accept the sounds as a background noise and will fail to listen. However, if the television or radio is switched on for selected programmes then the child will learn to listen. When the person looking after the child watches or listens too, they can talk about the programme together afterwards.

---

**Find out the names of the television and radio programmes for the under-fives. Watch or listen to one of them. Write about the ways in which the programme could help to expand the language of a three-year-old.**

---

Selective television viewing and radio listening can expand a child's experience and knowledge. In her imagination she can go on a boat trip or a train journey, or ride on a camel.

Words that have more than one meaning can be more easily explained if put into a song or game. The word 'turn' has several different meanings, e.g. 'turn on the radio', 'turn around' and 'it is your turn'. These different meanings can confuse a child. Children's television programmes often present in a visual and enjoyable way the various meanings of one word.

Later on in this chapter you will read more about talking and listening in the first years at school.

## Pre-school groups

The years before a child is five years old are often referred to as the pre-school years. During this time parents, brothers, sisters and all of those people who are close to the child will have played a considerable part in widening the child's knowledge, influencing her behaviour, developing her language and improving her skills.

There is a widespread view that if children under five years have some form of pre-school education then they will gain more benefit from their primary school education. It is not possible for all children to have pre-school education because there are not enough places available. Duncan, Simon,

Hazel, Heather and Milton are all of pre-school age and live in a large city suburb.

*Playgroups*

Duncan lived in a high-rise flat. His mother was worried about the fact that he was not mixing with other children of his age. The health visitor told her that a playgroup was held each Tuesday and Thursday morning from 9.30 – 12.00 in the nearby church hall. She suggested that the mother and child should go along and see if there was a vacancy.

During her visit to the playgroup Duncan's mother found out quite a lot about the Pre-school Playgroups Association. When the playgroup first started it was given a grant of money by the Pre-school Playgroups Association to help buy toys. A group of mothers held several jumble sales and with the money that they raised they bought a climbing frame, a doll's house and some large jigsaw puzzles.

Before permission was given for the play-group to be held in the church hall the Social Services department of the local authority sent one of their team to inspect the hall. This was to ensure that there were no health or safety risks. The Social Services department also said that in view of the number of toilets available and the size of the hall not more than twenty-five children were to attend at one time.

Mrs Norton, who was in charge of the play-group, said that a child had moved away that week and it was possible for Duncan to start. She explained that a small charge was made each week and that Duncan's mother, along with other mothers and fathers, was to take it in turns to help her.

Duncan's mother enjoys her involvement in the playgroup. Meeting other parents and talking over her worries has been a great help to her. 'I know a lot more about what to look for when choosing toys for Duncan and about the importance of a regular story time. Duncan is talking a lot better and is mixing more happily with other children. Before we came here he would not let me out of his sight. Duncan loves the water and sand. We just don't have the room in our small flat for sand trays.'

*Playbus*

Simon was an energetic three-and-a-half-year-old. His mother tried to get him into the playgroup but there were no vacancies. A neighbour suggested that his mother should try and get Simon a place in the pre-school group that met each Monday and Friday morning in the playbus. The bus parked on the edge of the play area of the nearby estate. It was an old double-decker bus that had been converted. The local Social Services department had bought it, stripped it of its seats and refitted it as a play area. Mrs Deakin was in charge of the bus and was helped by mothers on a rota basis. The play-bus moved to different districts on various days of the week. This gave more children access to its facilities.

Simon's mother said, 'The playbus has been a great help. It parks near so that I can easily get there. There were just too many children for the playgroup at the church hall. Simon was getting to the stage where he needed children of his own age to play with. I really do enjoy having a little time away from him in the week. He needed so much of my attention I was getting quite exhausted. We both benefit from the break away from each other.'

## Day nurseries

Hazel's mother was a single parent. Hazel was now one-and-a-half years old and, although her grandmother had been looking after her since she was born, she was beginning to find it too much for her. Sandra, Hazel's mother, was a secretary. She wanted to keep working because she enjoyed the company and her salary enabled her to have her own flat.

It was a great relief when Sandra heard that there was at last a vacancy at the day nursery. Day nurseries are run by the Social Services department of the local authority. They provide day care for small babies and children up to school age. They are intended to help parents who for various reasons cannot care for their children during the day.

The day nursery opened at eight o'clock in the morning so that Sandra was able to leave Hazel on her way to work. Sandra said, 'I have no worries about Hazel now. Of course the nursery will not take her if she is ill but fortunately my mother has said she would help me out then. I collect her on my way home from work, I'm usually there about quarter to six. They are open all the year round except Bank Holidays. I have to pay each week, but as the amount is related to my income it's not too much, and less than I would have to pay a good childminder. There are nursery nurses and student nursery nurses who help look after the children. There are plenty of play facilities there. They feed the children, change their nappies and generally keep them warm and safe. They really look after Hazel well.'

## Nursery schools

As soon as Heather was born her mother put her name down at the local nursery school for a place. Heather's mother had two other children who had both been to nursery school and she thought that they had settled into infant school quicker and made better progress with their number and language work as a result of this.

When Heather was three years old her

A day nursery.

mother was notified that there was a place available. There were so many children waiting for places that the head teacher of the nursery school arranged for one group of children to attend in the morning and another group to attend in the afternoon. This meant that twice as many children could benefit from nursery school experience.

The nursery school was the responsibility of the local education authority. The head teacher was a trained infant teacher and was helped by several trained nursery teachers.

Heather's mother was pleased that her daughter was able to have nursery school experience. 'I appreciate the fact that I don't have to pay. Heather only attends in term time so that she is at home with her sisters in the holidays. I know not all children are ready to be separated from their parents at three years old but Heather was happy to be away from me. She really looks forward to it. She does a lot of work that helps with word recognition like matching shapes, jigsaw puzzles and word games. Some part of each morning there is number work. They sing number rhymes, play number games and even do some weighing and measuring — with help of course.'

*Child minders*

When Milton was two-and-a-half years old his mother decided to return to work. Milton's mother was a single parent and she had no relatives living near. A friend suggested to her that she got in touch with the local Social Services department as they had a list of registered Child Minders. She was advised to leave Milton with a registered minder because this meant that someone from the Social Services department had visited the home and made sure that it was a suitable environment in which to care for other peoples' children.

After visiting three registered Child Minders, Milton's mother decided to leave him with Mrs Lockwood. Before making her decision, Milton's mother discussed with Mrs Lockwood how much she had to pay her, the number of hours that Milton was to be left for, and the meals that were to be provided. She also asked to see the garden and the toys.

After two weeks at Mrs Lockwood's Milton's mother said 'He has settled in well. I visited six times with Milton before I started work so that he got to know Mrs Lockwood. I like the calm way that she deals with the children. She is happy and firm and spends a lot of time talking and playing with the children. There are two other children there too, one three years and one four years old. She will not take Milton when he is unwell though because she says that it is not fair on the other children. I always try to be on time to collect him and let her know if I am going to be late.'

## Starting school

Carl is five years old and started school at the beginning of the term. It had not been possible to get Carl a place at nursery school or playgroup. His parents worried about how he would cope with the transition from home to school.

Before he started at Springfield Infants School his father had taken him on three visits to the school during term time. He met his teacher, Ms Counsell, and was allowed to stay for the morning and play with the toys. His mother said, 'I think he was a bit apprehensive at first but I took him to buy new shoes and a warm shirt for school. He seemed to start looking forward to it then. If I was out shopping I would always try to be near the school when the children came out so that he could see the mothers meeting their children. Before he started I made sure that he could tie his laces and do up his buttons and zips. The first morning I was allowed to stay for a while, that also helped.'

Some parents think that once a child starts school, they have no part to play in their child's learning. They believe that schools are entirely responsible for the education of children. During the early school years a child's attitude to school will be very much shaped by the interest and encouragement shown by their parents. Children's interest in books and stories will increase when they start school and for some time yet they will continue to enjoy being read to.

Starting school for many five-year-old children is the beginning of a great new adventure and this is how it should be and continue to be.

## The first two years at school

In Britain most children start school at the age of five. When children start school they go into the first class or reception class. Children starting school bring with them a variety of skills and experiences.

A person visiting an infant school will have the impression that most of the time is spent playing. You will remember that play is an important part of a child's life.

The activities that take place in an infant class are ones that will:

develop skills and concepts that have already been learnt

give a range of new experiences

develop new skills

---

**Listed below are some skills and concepts that will be taught and developed. Complete the list.**

---

| Skill or concept | Toy game activity | Value to the child |
|---|---|---|
| Recognition of shape | Jigsaw puzzles | To help distinguish between shapes to assist with reading and writing |
| Weight | | |
| Number | | |
| Word recognition | | |
| Hand/eye co-ordination | | |
| Concentration | | |
| Recognising and distinguishing between sounds | | |

---

## Learning to read

A child cannot learn to read or write until she has mastered certain basic skills. She must be able to:

see the difference between similar shapes, e.g. b/c,u/v,m/n,d/b

follow with her eyes from left to right

tell the difference between sounds

hold and control a pencil

During the first school years a good deal of time is spent acquiring and perfecting these skills.

## Children's drawings

When a child draws she is not only using her imagination and creative skills but her hand/eye co-ordination and learning to control her fingers and hands.

Children's drawings change considerably during the first two years at school. By five years most children will be able to draw people. They draw them with big round heads, small bodies and matchstick arms and legs.

*Learning to get on with other people*

You will remember from Chapter 7 that this is called socialisation. For many children the infant school will provide their first experience of being a member of a large group. At first there may be quarrels and tears because the children will have many new relationships and experiences to cope with such as:

sharing toys

sharing the teacher with twenty-nine other children

having to be quiet and attentive and not disturb others

having to consider the feelings of many others

The child will need to be allowed to experiment and try out different kinds of behaviour. For instance, playing games which have rules. (The rules may be hard to stick to, but a child who learns to follow them will get on better with her classmates.)

*Learning to be independent*

Many parents will have helped their children to achieve independence in ways that will enable them to cope with everyday situations at school. Children easily become worried and distressed if they experience difficulty coping with tasks such as:

lacing shoes

pulling up zips

going to the toilet alone

distinguishing between the front and back of a garment

being able to tell the left shoe from the right one

At infant school children are encouraged to

carry out these simple tasks for themselves.

*Talking and listening*

The foundations of language will be laid before the child starts school. In the infant school a good deal of time is spent expanding children's language. There will be opportunities to:

listen to stories and look at books
ask questions
listen to answers

Not all the children in the infant school will be at the same stage of development; some children will be able to do things before others. The emphasis is on stimulating the child, that is, providing her with opportunities to learn and valuing and rewarding her achievements.

# Index